Retail is more than margins and products;
Retail is fun, passion and creating the ultimate experience
for your customers!

Enjoy Oil & Vinegar, Enjoy retail and have a great 2005!

PASSIONATE ABOUT TASTE

OIL & VINEGAR HEAD OFFICE: KOOPVAARDIJWEG 19B 4906 CV OOSTERHOUT THE NETHERLANDS
T. +31 (0)162 472060 F. +31 (0)162 463138 W. WWW. OILVINEGAR.COM

Retail
Branding

MICHEL VAN TONGEREN

Retail Branding

From
stopping
power to
shopping
power

BIS Publishers,
Amsterdam

Retail is not about shops and stores. It's about a one-to-one relationship between companies and real people, in which the company becomes a person and the encounter a conversation.

MICHEL VAN TONGEREN

Originally trained as an industrial designer at the
Gerrit Rietveld Academy, Michel van Tongeren and
two others started the company svt Branding +
Design Group. Intrigued by the increased profes-
sionalism of English retail companies, he switched
the field of focus from industrial design to retail
design. Now, after working in the retail business
for almost 20 years, the company is one of the few
in the Netherlands specialized in retail branding
and retail design. As Director of Branding and
Strategy he is an appreciated lecturer at seminars,
conferences and universities.

svt Branding + Design Group has worked for
ABN-AMRO bank, Ahold, KPN retail, Miss Etam,
Delhaize and Kingfisher, among others.

www.svt.nl
retailbranding@planet.nl

A short while ago I was on a fishing trip to a remote area of central South America. The nearest town, a one-hour bone breaking drive away, sported a surprisingly well-stocked general store although not much else. A feature of the store was an artless sign in Pidgin English which translated as: "all your favourite brands at discount prices."

Before fishing, I was in New York, where the smartest SoHo and Village shops were offering their sophisticated and wealthy customers much the same as their Belizean counterpart, namely, "favourite brands at lowest prices."

The frame that holds these disparate shopping experiences are the two great imperatives of contemporary retailing: price and brands. Price is perhaps for another time; meanwhile this important book deals most fulsomely with the phenomenon that is retail branding.

In the post-industrial age, if you want a mirror on contemporary society look at retailing: dominant brands mirror how we feel about ourselves; successful locations describe modern demographics and population shifts; at the beginning of the twenty first century the contemporary Russian retail scene speaks as eloquently about that society as did those images a decade ago of the wall coming down.

For shopping is not only at the cutting edge of the democratic imperative of choice, but a primary leisure occupation and the major underpinning of modern urban life. Recognising these facts is often troublesome for the anti-consumerist lobby. But when President Bush can urge a post 9/11 traumatised America not to be downhearted but to "enjoy yourselves, go shopping" it must be clear that retailing transcends mere consumption and occupies a position that in any national way of life is sociological and political as well as economic.

Perhaps it has been increasingly so ever since the first Department Stores began to change everything about shopping in the middle of the 19th century. Ben Franklin once famously observed that only two things in life are certain: "death and taxes". He could have added a third certainty, change, and in the murderously competitive and endlessly inventive world of retailing, the changes – ushered in firstly by the Department Store revolution, followed by such innovations as multiple stores, supermarkets, and shopping centres – have kept the fires of competition red hot. And no industry, perhaps with the exception of active sports, is so dominated by brand culture.

Shopping has become the focus for like-minded people and shops are there to provide the customer with branded goods which act as symbols of like-mindedness. Retailers all over the world operate in a world of complexities and contradictions wherein consumers often feel alienated. Brand attachment or rejection gives the consumer the opportunity for self-expression and personal decision taking. Where even the African, leading the simplest of lives somewhere in Africa, knows the difference between Manchester United or Ajax, Levi's or Wrangler.

It would of course be overbold to suggest that brands, and in particular retail brands, hold the meaning of life! To the questions of why are we here? where are we going? there are no answers, only uncertainties. But the modern shopper's relationship with brands at least helps provide a small comfort within the big mystery, for brands help anchor a tiny island of familiarity and understanding in a wider sea of uncertainty. Why are we so attracted to brands? The question is often answered either in contemporary psycho babble or alternatively in those very human terms of tribalism, territory and loyalties, but the brand encounter and its strategic management and manipulation is very much more complex than this. Michel writes eloquently and knowledgeably and from experience about how to measure and manage the brand for maximum benefit to retailer and consumer alike.

In recent years, ever inventive, retailers have been in the vanguard of customer and product management through strategic branding. This book then is timely. It sets out to explain to both professional and layman alike in a clear and approachable manner the power, the prejudices and the experiences that lie behind the phenomenal growth of retail branding during the last couple of decades. The author's insights spring from a lifetime in professional practice and the book is filled with helpful insights and splendidly relevant examples.

Without doubt the customers' preoccupation with brands, as is the nature with all things in retail, will change. King Brand is dead, long live King what? No doubt in due course Michel will tell us and I for one can't wait; but in the meantime the thoughts in this book on brands, shops and shopping, on the why and the how, are long overdue. Some of these thoughts are very, very original, others good common sense; but isn't common sense the very essence of good retailing?

Rodney Fitch CBE PPCSD,
London

ACKNOWLEDGEMENTS

This book on strategic retail branding and formula development has grown apace with the evolution of our company over the past 15 years from a pure design agency into a branding and design agency. The knowledge in this book has accordingly been built upon our continual desire to understand how things work and how we could move from design as the objective to design as the means, in order to represent the personality of the brands of our clients on the one hand and to link up with the consumer through inspiring and functional (retail) concepts on the other.

Retail is a rewarding topic in as far as that goes. Because it is in such constant flux and is a direct representation of 'who we are', 'how we live' and 'what we are thinking', set in the spirit of the times.

A brand must constantly innovate, keep renewing itself in order to remain relevant for the consumer. With retail this is also continually measurable in the reactions and appreciation of the consumer and is in essence more simple than for a product brand, because stores enter into a real, active relationship with their customers. In that respect design cannot be seen separately from the constant innovation and development of the formula, because it gives shape to the underlying core values that ultimately offer brand distinction to the customer. Otherwise design can only take on the competition by setting trends, after which it will be replaced by even newer trends.

Our mainspring and ambition is therefore to professionalize design, separate it from 'the artiste', and let it be the creative representation of the interplay of the rational and emotional elements of the brand and its formula. In order to do this well it is necessary to have a deep understanding of how (retail) brands work, how the formulas are organized and established and what people expect from the brand.

This book primarily presents a view of the subject of Retail Branding and retail formula development, over which very little has been written and very little research has been done until now. And although we have discovered, distinguished and described some basic values, this view is a snapshot that will develop further in time and along with the times. The reason for this book therefore is to set down that body of ideas and have it serve as a departure point for the development of further professionalization of the field.

This book is first of all meant for all those involved in this field, from retailers pur sang to marketers and designers, but because we in Western society almost all come in daily contact with stores, this book is in fact meant for everyone. In imitation of the fantastic title of Paco Underhill's book 'Why We Buy', this book could also be called 'Why We Shop', or even better, 'Why Do We Shop There?'

This book would not have come about without my partner Laurent Vollebregt, with whom I founded SVT Branding & Design Group 15 years ago, because throughout the years he has constantly challenged and encouraged me to take the next step, thereby creating the necessary space for me to do so. My thanks for this.

I also wish to thank Gwendolin Majoor, without whom this book would never have come about either. As brand researcher and editor she has managed the enormous task of taking the basis of my story and steadily developing and amplifying it in a very inspired manner and with tremendous dedication into what has become, in my view, a very readable story.

Furthermore, I thank Frank Schoeman and Hoyte de Ranitz, my (design) partners of a later date, as well as all of our current employees and those of the past, from whom I have learnt very much, all in all. And also the designers, design agencies and brand thinkers who have gone before us and remain an inspiration. That's why I am also so proud that Rodney Fitch, one of the founding fathers of the profession, was prepared to write the foreword for this book.

Finally, this book would never have come into being without all of the clients for whom we have worked during the past years; entrepreneurs for whom I have infinite respect and in who I remain immensely interested. In this connection I would like to mention Wilfred van Es in particular, the founder of the chain store Fooks, who gave our agency its first chance to develop along with a real chain and from which I gained the fundamentals of my retail knowledge.

I dedicate this book to my brother Peter (†).

Michel van Tongeren
Amsterdam

01
Retail Therapy Ahead

THE MEDICINAL EFFECTS OF SHOPPING

As a way of fighting boredom or a bad mood, of spending time with friends or seeking self-assurance, shopping has become a sort of self-medication that is practised by people in all walks of life. The person who thought up the sign 'Retail Therapy Ahead' (hanging at Luton Airport in 2001) understood this. The phrase speaks volumes about our daily life in Western society.

Therapy such as this is not only for the shopaholics who can't go a day without shopping. Even those who work in the retail business or are connected with it in one way or another and thus know how it works are led by the same feelings. Perhaps sometimes consciously, but often quite unconsciously. For you can indulge yourself with shopping, you can compensate for your displeasure, and you can show the world who you are by the stores you shop at and the products (brands) you buy.

Now, one person might be more sensitive to brands and more consciously busy with them than another, but the fact remains that in our present-day society there's no longer any escaping them. And although branding began with products, today virtually everything is branded: stores, services, enterprises, cities, countries, even people.

THE ORIGIN OF BRANDING

The origin of the word 'brand' comes from its literal meaning in Old English: 'to burn'. In other words, to mark by a hot iron, as with the branding of animals. Initially, a brand was meant to indicate which farmer the cows or horses belonged to, a mark of ownership. And then such a brand also became a mark of quality. Cows from a particular farmer were better, stronger, tastier than others and therefore became popular and more desirable than others.

The farmer who owned those exceptional cows let them graze in special pastures, made sure that they led a stress-free cow's life and gave all of them a name of their own. At a certain point word of this got around and more and more people started talking about it. As a result, the farmer could slap a stiff price tag on his cows – but they were worth it, too. For the cattle dealers at the market, choosing now became easier. At one glance, that farmer's brand stood for quality, it was a safe choice. And once the dealers met the farmer, he actually turned out to be the amiable sort of man you'd expect to be associated with such quality. It all fit, he was genuine.

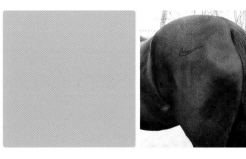

Race horse

Sign at Luton Airport (UK) in 2001

This subsequently made itself felt further on down the chain, for when you served your guests a steak from one of those cows, that excellent choice reflected upon you as a host. Apart from the fact that the steak tasted delicious, its origin (and especially the story that was involved) made this steak extra special. It had conversational value.

The brand on the cow stood for both rational and emotional value. The rational value sprang from the quality of breeding and care of the animals and the good taste of the meat which was a result of that. The emotional value was the status you acquired when you served the meat to your guests.

The emotional aspect thus revolves around who the originator is and what he stands for, or in other words, who is behind the brand and what it does for you as a buyer.

WHY DO WE BRAND?

When there was hardly any question of middlemen or distributors as yet, brands were not necessary. The craftsman or manufacturer was in direct contact with his customers. And he could deliver products made exactly according to the wishes of the end-user.

After the mass production of goods became possible, production was concentrated and distributors became necessary. Direct contact between the producer and consumer vanished; now it was the retailer who had a relationship with the end-user. So producers started branding their products, for a branded package was a guarantee of quality and made it possible to have contact with the target group and acquire name recognition.

You might say that the first industrialists were the new 'anonymous', who were searching for ways of transmitting information to the end-user. In doing so, they took hardly any account of the wishes and needs of the many small independent distributors. Theirs was a 'push' strategy. The distributor was the intermediary who had to put forward and sell the products of producers as cheaply as possible to as many end-users as possible.

That changed in Europe in the 70s. Production techniques were refined and improved, prosperity increased and competition accordingly sharpened. By now consumers could choose from an increasingly broad supply of goods, so that producers found it more and more difficult to sell their products. The market shifted from a seller's market to a buyer's market. This period saw the refinement of many marketing tools (advertising, market research, 'branding', etc.), which could be used to bypass the retail trade and communicate directly with the consumer.

A number of years later the power held by producers began to diminish rapidly. Through expansion of scale, concentration and centralization, but also through the increased market awareness of distributors, the distribution range grew – and with it, the power of distributors. The roles had been reversed. Now it was the distributors who chose which producers/suppliers they wanted to do business with.

So now producers had to focus their marketing on two target groups. One strategy was aimed at end-users, with the objective of creating added demand for the product (pull). And another strategy was aimed at distributors, which usually consisted of support for their marketing activities. Producers focused more and more on product development: In an oversaturated market, products had become taken for granted and people were demanding a broader, more varied, more innovative and higher-quality selection. In the meantime, we are now seeing more collaboration between producers and distributors, so that the total way of thinking and dealing has become much more customer oriented.

Customers don't choose products on the basis of price or effectiveness; instead, they ask themselves: "What sort of dinner set defines me as a person?"

The narrator in the movie 'The Fight Club'

Apart from the original reason for brands, which is still their essential basis, brands have acquired another, very important function for people in the West. With the disintegration of traditional society, people started looking for new selection criteria, denominators that identify you and make it possible for others to 'place' you. This makes life safer – for after all, most of us are security seekers who yearn for some means of confirmation. Such brand identification and the like-mindedness between the users of brands is the idea behind the Dutch dating site www.branddating.nl. On that site you use brand preferences to describe yourself and the person you're looking for – the new way to search for your ideal mate.

Dutch dating website, where you can meet others by describing yourself with brands

Certain brands suit you, and that helps make life a bit easier: you don't have to think about every purchase eachtime you go to the supermarket.

The retail business is the largest industry in the world; more people work in it than in any other industry. Strangely enough, specific knowledge pertaining to retail branding is not widely available. Naturally there are schools at which such knowledge is on the course program (albeit indirectly); but experience shows that too little is done with it. The driving force behind many decisions is entrepreneurship and impulsiveness, commerciality (the cost aspect) and gut feelings, instead of *additionally* looking at the aspect of content. The word 'additionally' is used expressly here, because without financial considerations and especially not without emotions and trial & error, exciting concepts and ideas would never make it to the market. However, a lucky shot alone is not enough; the foundation must be established and substantiated.

This is why the phrase 'Retail Therapy Ahead' also applies to the industry, which should always be looking for methods and means of improving itself. Retail is an industry that is developing at incredible speed and yet one that is relatively averse to theorizing and strategic thinking. And when it does apply theory, this usually entails the traditional marketing models, which are not only outmoded, but also primarily directed toward the producers' side. These models pay no attention to the emotional side – how shopping works and how a company with truly unique values can differentiate itself. It is necessary to build up and develop new knowledge that is specifically about retail. Even a relatively simple model, such as will be discussed in chapter 7, can provide much added insight.

It is time to question the basic thinking behind brand management. It was created in different market conditions, different situations, and has been re-diffused time after time in brand management textbooks. Strategic wisdom warns: if it is taught, then it is probably obsolete; since the essence of good brand management is differentiation, advanced brand management should break free from the classic brand management moulds or at least not hesitate to question their relevance.

Jean-Noël Kapferer

Besides being large, the retail business is very old. The first forms of retail date back to many centuries before Christ. But it has only been a short while since large-scale marketing of stores and chain stores began. The biggest retail concern in the world for instance, Wal-Mart, is a very young company just 40 years old, founded by Sam Walton in 1962. His principles, revolutionary at the time, are still held ever high: 'strive for excellence', 'service to our customers' (including 'every day low price') and 'respect for the individual'.

While one company might be highly successful, another will have greater difficulties keeping its head above water. For retailing is not simple, and many enterprises die young. We can probably all think of a few chain stores from our youth that have now vanished. In a changing society, they no longer could fulfil a relevant and essential role. Evidently Wal-Mart is doing something right, 'something' that lets them continually renew their hold on the market. We will go into 'surviving' in more depth later.

In any case, as a retailer you always have to be on your toes. Self reflection, theoretical and strategic thinking and adaptive tactical action are necessary in order to be successful in our present-day, rapidly changing society; and it is essential to get a grip on the ever ambivalent consumer.

As yet, very little has been written on branding in general and retail branding in particular. Many books that claim to be about branding actually describe normal marketing processes. But what, in fact, is the difference between products and retail, between branding and marketing, between a product brand and a retail brand? How do retail brands originate, how do they work and how can they be given direction? This book will attempt to answer these questions. Next we will examine the translation of brands into concepts that appeal to a targeted group of buyers. And we will examine designing, the translation of ideas into tangible, visible, audible, tasteable and smellable surroundings and objects – which also have to be designed so that they are affordable and adaptable to the times.

Marketing communicates quickly and single-mindedly, branding is slow and multi-faceted.

Jacques Chevron (founding partner of JCR&A)

PEOPLE AND BRANDS

A contribution from Wim Buffing, coordinator/teacher at the School of Economics Inholland, department of Retail Management & Small Business to Consumers

Groups

People are group creatures. Therefore we all belong to various groups, some of which are formed on the basis of tradition or friendship, for example, while others come together more coincidentally. In addition to these more or less fixed and acknowledged groups, people form various temporary or semi-temporary groups or coalitions throughout the day. For instance when you work with someone for a short time or when you exchange a few words with the person sitting opposite you in the train, and so forth.

Risk-avoiding behaviour

People can fulfil a different role in each of these groups. At home you might be known as the life of the party, at work you keep a somewhat lower profile and amongst your friends you're the one who knows everything about motorcycles. Belonging to a group is a way of surviving – for loneliness not infrequently leads to death. That fear unites people. Usually this drive to find and maintain a place within a group is not conscious, it's more of an instinctive and therefore fundamental need. Which is why people display risk-avoiding behaviour. They will not jeopardize their acquired position without good reason. For unlike 'danger', which is something that happens to you, risks can be calculated and therefore possibly avoided. A characteristic property of groups is that each has its own codes and norms (even very temporary or very small groups). These are not put into

words, naturally, but the members of the group think that they know them.

Brands

The general function of brands in today's society is that they replace familiar social reference points that have fallen away. Education and background, religion and culture – none of these provide unequivocal clues for placing a person any more. Partly because of secularisation, other rules and agreements now apply and people are beginning to regroup. Moreover, we are very visually oriented nowadays. Brands are physical, you can see them plainly, as opposed to the religion people believe in or the family they come from. Matters which were much more important in the past and more widely known.

In groups that have already existed for a long time or that are very closely knit (the family and very good friends), brands will probably play a more limited role. At least, you will not be judged because of them. Brands will always provide matter for conversation in such groups, however. Group members copy one another's behaviour (that is, brands) because they trust one another, or drop brands because one of them has had a bad experience with it and talked about it at length.

In groups whose members are still feeling each other out to some extent and in which there is a somewhat stronger hierarchy, brands can play a role in justifying behaviour and limiting risks. To that end, people will consciously or unconsciously try to assess their behaviour by judging it through the eyes and ears of their reference group, in other words, reflective behaviour. For instance, defending your cooking skills with a remark like: "But I got it from Jamie Oliver!" or "No…this comes from Carrefour!"

One also sees that the person known in the group for being inspirational or innovative can easily introduce new things, such as music, books, or a new brand (new for the group, at least). Her good taste is appreciated and followed. Most of the time this person has learned or copied it from a group in which she is more of a follower. In this way we all play together a complex game of conforming, trying things out, selecting, and profiling ourselves. A game without regulations, but certainly with very many rules.

Retail Brands

Retail brands create a tangible context and 'measurable' added value. When a store is wellspring of conversation, it will have value for a group, and then the store can become a 'must' for the members of that group. In addition, a store can fulfil a symbolic function. You could almost consider it a new group that you can join. The store then becomes an important group member, as it were. But it is not a real group. You don't have to justify your behaviour to the retail brand, which is an added advantage.

Loyalty

Whether or not we are talking about product brands or retail brands, people always have associations with brands. Roughly speaking, the core associations are the first two or three slogans that pop up in a person's mind when he thinks of the (retail) brand. When these associations are positive, then most likely he is loyal to the brand, or in any case the brand plays a role in

his life.

Brand owners, especially owners of strong brands, try to steer this network of associations in order to ensure that people remember certain positive brand characteristics. This is comparable to the behaviour of important members of a group: the rest of the group expect them to address and inspire the group every now and then.

As soon as a brand attracts negative attention, or people have a bad experience with it, the associations are negative and consumers will simply step over to another alternative, for there are plenty of them, after all.

People are group creatures and always will be. As a result, they are continually occupied with reducing the risk of not belonging to any group. For the majority of the population, this is the most important drive.

Wim Buffing

02
The
Marketplace

This is the marketplace – literally and figuratively. And this is the target group. And that's all that you know about your target group, in fact. Market and consumer research can provide depth, of course, you can distinguish various target groups and analyze their buying behaviour based on customer charge cards, but in fact you can only look at them like in the photo, from above and from afar.

WHAT DO YOU KNOW ABOUT YOUR TARGET GROUP? (NOTHING, REALLY.)

Because the target group is different in the morning than in the afternoon, different on Mondays than on Saturdays, different in the spring than in the fall. The people walking there are individuals. They even feel differently every hour and behave accordingly, are for instance extrovert at one moment and crawl into their shell at the next, behave differently in a group than when alone, and are different again when in couples.

Why do people buy from a particular flower vendor?

Consumer profiles are not static. Depending on the time of the week, or day, a consumer can assume a different consumer profile.

Stephen Anderson (retail designer at BDP)

WHY DO PEOPLE BUY AT A SPECIFIC PLACE?

Why are they there? Have they come for the flower market or for the cozy little cafés which probably line the square? Have they come for the cathedral (this is the location of Dom in Milan) or are they simply crossing the square on their way home? You can't tell by looking at them. Why do they buy flowers and plants at that particular spot? Not because of the plants. You can buy them everywhere, and they are more or less the same everywhere – the differences in quality and price are negligible. No, they buy there because of the location, the ambience and the mood they're in.

And why do they buy from a particular salesperson? Sometimes it appears as if it's by chance and sometimes it's indeed by chance, but in most cases people are attracted by a combination of personality and presentation. They pick out a merchant who clearly demonstrates his identity, usually in an imperceptible manner and without being conscious of it himself. Such clarity derives from the choices a merchant makes – from his person, his feeling for the market and the product he offers. And also simply because he has chosen that specific spot for its *umfeld*, because he feels at home there. In other words, only after a retailer chooses a course and thus makes himself eligible can people choose him. That is the basis of every (retail) brand.

Only after a retailer chooses a course and thus makes himself eligible can people choose him. That is the basis of every (retail) brand.

Zoom in on one person and you lose sight of the rest

'Making yourself eligible' is not the same as 'focusing on a target group'. By making yourself eligible, people who feel attracted to your way of doing things almost automatically come to you. If you explicitly focus on one target group, you shut people out beforehand. The picture of the wall with many faces tells the story. They are all different people and it is difficult to find any relation between them or to predict which of them will visit your shop. On the other hand, when you zoom in on one, you no longer see the others. That's why we say: Do things your own way, show who you are, make clear choices, and then let people choose you.

BE ELIGIBLE

Back to the flower market, because that example makes several things clear. Clearer than a shopping street could, in the first instance. All of the goods and merchants on this marketplace can be compared at a glance. The factors that need to be considered and compared are simple and relatively objective – freshness of the product, variety, price, and so forth. Moreover, the similarities between what is on offer are greater than the differences – it's a relatively generic supply. With this particular market, it also holds true that the presentation of goods is for the most part similar.

But consumers still have to make choices, and all that they can do is accept the decisions that the merchants have already made and then proceed from there:

- pricing, no matter how small differences may be
- specialism – one merchant will feature a broad range of products, while another might be totally specialized in fuchsias
- presentation – one stall will look like a potpourri, another will be ordered according to size or colour; one merchant will choose profusion, another restraint
- and finally, the personality of the merchant and his employees play a role.

In short: Product, price, look and feel are the denominators upon which consumers can base their choices. What's more, their involvement at a particular moment and place with a particular product and the importance that they attach to the purchase are also determining factors.

Today in the product arena and in the political arena, you have to have a position. There are too many competitors out there. You can't win by not making enemies, by being everything to everybody. To win in today's competitive environment, you have to go out and make friends, carve out a specific niche in the market. Even if you lose a few doing so.

Al Ries and Jack Trout (advertising strategists)

THE MARKETPLACE VERSUS THE SHOPPING STREET

The above is true, at any rate, for a relatively simple situation like the marketplace. In a shopping street the set of choices is more difficult to establish. It requires more effort for a consumer to discover whether a particular shop will be appropriate for her, for her desires and her mood – she will have to go inside to find out. You wouldn't so readily walk into six flower shops in order to compare them, the way you easily can do on a market. Because of this a shop has to immediately arouse a consumer's interest (or be already known) before she will take the trouble to go inside.

A retailer must therefore purposefully attract the customer's attention, establishing the initial contact through outstore communications and after that through the physical store and the look & feel of the whole. Whereas on the marketplace a merchant can look at people, make jokes, sing the praises of his goods, and try to make direct contact.

The similarity between the marketplace and the shopping street lies in the fact that they both must launch a two-stage rocket: first attract attention, then bind through personality. The difference lies in how they attract attention. Merchants on the marketplace can immediately do this through their personality. A shop can only reveal its personality at a later stage. However, 'binding'(with the market stall + merchant or the retail brand can only occur when the seller's personality fits with your own personality.

Professor Rob van der Kind has developed a theory partially based on this same principle. A retailer, he maintains, can only realize a turnover after he first attracts the attention of consumers through the external marketing mix. The external marketing mix concentrates on arousing interest in the formula. On the one hand, mass media communications aimed at promoting the brand name and image must be put into effect. On the other hand, the store itself must have stopping power through its storefront, show windows, logo, site (around the store communications), etc. He calls this the attraction value of the store formula, which is analogous to the proposition that the store must first attract, stand out and entice in order to draw customers inside at all.

The second factor in realizing a turnover is the internal marketing mix (the transaction value) – converting the aroused interest into actual purchasing behaviour. This means that everything inside the store must be right: assortment, personnel, visual merchandising, store design, and so forth. And these days a store must also offer 'an experience', something a little extra. More about Professor van der Kind's theory can be found at the end of this chapter.

It is important not to underestimate the following step: 'binding with your personality', or living up to your promise. This is about turning buyers into lovers and ambassadors of your brand, people who are so enthusiastic about the store and its products that they tell all of their friends and acquaintances about it. To generate this mouth-to-mouth advertising, the store will need to have something which makes a lasting impression, something which people like to tell to others. That way you can guarantee – and increase – the loyalty of your group of buyers.

> Distinction (standing out) > Personality (binding)

ATTRACTING ATTENTION

The following is a telling example of this: You walk into a cafe and see a nice-looking person standing at the bar. Naturally you would rather look at him or her (or even better, talk to him or her) than someone who is not your type. If you do manage to strike up a conversation and he or she turns out to have a nice personality, you have every reason to continue the enjoyable experience. But if it turns out that this person has an unpleasant character, one that does not match yours, you quickly break off the conversation. It could also happen, of course, that you 'accidentally' meet someone who at first sight is not at all your type. Sometimes this can click unexpectedly well, even though it takes a bit more effort at first to see through the 'outer layer'. But the chance of making contact, the chance of success, is much smaller. It's exactly the same with a store. It must stand out, attract and seduce and then carry out its promise with true personality.

A store must stand out, attract and seduce and then carry out its promise with true personality.

ATTRACTION & TRANSACTION, A THEORY OF PROFESSOR ROB VAN DER KIND

from: 'Retailing: Why, How and What Next?',
internal company presentation, March 2000

Trade and Retail

As soon as product manufacturers deliver their goods to the sales channel (usually retailers), they realize returns. Retailers generate returns only when they resell to consumers. In trade marketing, a client is a client, and it is usually clear in advance who that client is. In retail, this is by no means always the case. Visitors who come into a store most certainly do not always go back out as customers (that is, as visitors who have bought something). Especially in a 'fun shopping' atmosphere, visitors regularly come in and look, but end up by not buying anything.

Therefore the first function of retail is to ensure that consumers can make the right choice from the possibly very wide variety of products at their disposal in an easy and pleasant manner (thus minimalizing the search costs).

Because of this, marketing has a different nature in retail than it does in trade. Van der Kind divides the retail marketing mix into what he calls the external marketing mix, or the attraction value of a store formula, and the internal marketing mix, or the transaction value of a store formula.

The External Marketing Mix

Attraction:
Creating interest in the formula. In other words, name recognition and image. The mix consists of:
- public (target group)
- place
- product (assortment)
- price
- promotion

The Internal Marketing Mix

Transaction:
Converting created interest into actual purchasing behaviour. That is, the effectiveness of the store as a sales machine. The mix consists of:
- presentation
- personnel
- physical distribution
- pricing structure
- productivity

By combining the attraction value and the transaction value, a formula for returns (R) can be obtained:

$$R = AC \times TI \times C \times RA$$

AC: area of coverage
TI: turnout index
C: conversion
RA: receipt amount

AC x TI stand for the attraction value, C x RA for the transaction value. To illustrate the power of such multiplication: the positive influencing of both components has a fortifying effect upon each of them. Conversely, underexposure of one of the components can wipe out the (positive) effect of the other.

03
Identity

MAKING THE DIFFERENCE WITH WHAT YOU'VE GOT

Nature is exceptionally beautiful in Japan. A feeling even came over me that nature is much more beautiful in Japan than elsewhere. Now, practically every country has its own specific type of nature, each with its own charms, yet in Japan it seemed even more beautiful, even more refined, more in balance. Nature simply is, you might say – and its true identity lies within itself. A company's identity is likewise a given. A company cannot simply assume another identity.

BRAND STRETCH

Yet there are ways of changing things. When you look carefully at this picture of the Japanese garden, you can discern a man in the tree at the above left. He is giving the Japanese nature a helping hand, making it more beautiful, cultivating it. In the same way, with just as much patience, dedication and money, a company's identity can also be changed. That is, if you know exactly what you want and call in the proper specialists. But be aware that just like with the huge bonsai trees, it takes an enormous amount of time.

The breathtaking beauty of nature in Japan. But how natural is it, in fact?

Instead of readjusting the identity, it is simpler to look for identity stretch; that is, the 'bandwidth' in which a company can comfortably operate. This is often more broad than originally thought. And although that bandwidth might be less broad for the 'simple' chain stores that can be found in every shopping street, in comparison to the extreme liberties that Prada takes with its store interiors it is still wide enough to undertake interesting – and preferably innovating – steps. As Sir Terence Conran has appropriately said, "People's taste develops by being shown something different."

The fact that such leeway indeed exists becomes clear by comparing the identity of a company with that of a person. A person adapts to different situations: You dress differently when you're on vacation than as a consultant at the office, you behave differently at a romantic dinner than when watching a football match, and most people will use different language in a café with their friends than at the dinner table of their inlaws (...the first time they meet, in any case). Yet you remain the same person 'in your mind'. This behaviour (adaptive behaviour, in other words) is necessary in order to survive. It is a reason for success. But it can also be a reason for failure; a person who adapts to no situation whatsoever is called 'ill-bred', sometimes even 'socially handicapped'. A company can also adapt, put on a different set of clothes, display different behaviour, as long as it remains the same 'in its mind'. Otherwise it will not come across as trustworthy and will not be accepted by consumers. For they know perfectly well whether something really comes from within or if it has been thought up and imposed. That's why it's logical that Prada can afford to do extreme things. Prada happens to have an extremely colourful identity.

An about-turn in identity is actually only accepted when it is the sign of great inner turmoil, just like with people.

Jos van der Zwaal (creative strategist)

THE COMPLETE PICTURE

In the last chapter we discussed the importance of attracting consumer attention and then binding it through personality. The strength of the brand or retail brand will be revealed when this attracting and binding occurs as a result of true identity. For displaying your true identity is your strength. That's why it's necessary to be aware of your identity before taking any steps. And your image in the market as well, for there must be a clear relation between the two. The company itself and every possible way in which a (future) customer can come in contact with it – the complete picture, let's say – must live and breathe its true identity. Only then will the image that you acquire in the market actually match your true character, the one you desire.

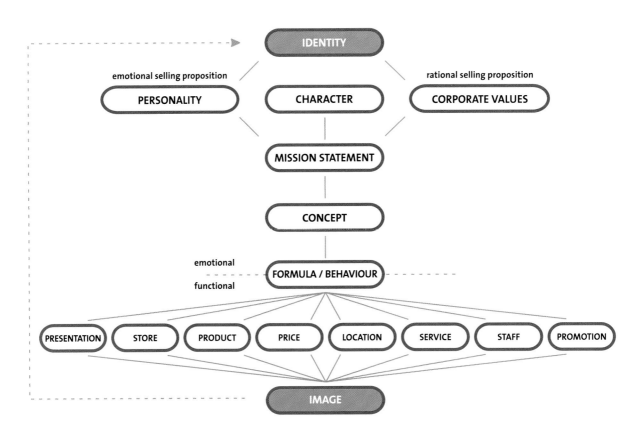

⊕ THE RETAIL FORMULA®

THE RETAILFORMULA®

The Retailformula® model gives a picture of the path between a company's identity and its image in the market. At the top of the model is the identity, an inextricable part of a company. It's who you are. In addition to the ambitions, this comprises a rational and an emotional component. 'Rational' refers to what it is and how it works, and 'emotional' refers to who the sender is and what that does for the buyer. At the bottom of the model is the image, or in other words, how you are perceived by the market. You could say that the success formula lies between these two extremes.

Advertising, if it is any good, should help to confirm what already is, not what should be.

Scott Bedbury (brand consultant)

When we take a look at identity, it often turns out that the emotional component tends to be forgotten. When a company lists its strong points, the unique selling propositions (USPs), this usually only includes the RSPs, the rational selling propositions. In other words, the business values, which in many cases can be copied. Whereas consumers base the majority of their decisions about becoming, being, or remaining customers on emotionality, non-rationality.

For example, your store could be the first to carry hip orange T-shirts, but there's a good chance that within two weeks every store on street will be selling orange T-shirts. How do you manage to get consumers to keep buying the shirt from you nevertheless?

The crux of the matter is the added value that comes with the shirt, added value that stems from the combination of product (or service) and personality. It is the fingerprint of the organization and it is what makes that T-shirt different from the shirts of other suppliers. So it is advisable to get a grip on the emotional aspect of the company and communicate this externally and internally.

The brand concept is developed from identity (including the emotional and rational values), positioning and ambition and/or market vision. It is the starting point for the formula, the stretch of the brand and the organization. For with a successful formula all brand expressions come from one source, and the organization emanates brand in everything it does. This is called 'living the brand', a term that you often come across these days. In chapter 9 we will go into the brand concept in depth.

The brand concept take shape in the formula elements, which constitute a link to the image. When the translation of the brand concept into the elements of the formula is right, your image matches your identity, because the consumer picks up the proper values.

In theory this sounds simple, but the reality is difficult to capture in a model. A great number of steps between the idea and the reality will still need to be taken. The following example can help clarify the importance of identity and show that its relation to image can be stronger than thought.

Long ago we were commissioned to work on the visual strength of a brand of jeans. The brand was a strong player in the local market because of the product's good quality and perfect fit, notably for women. In our naivete we gleefully began collecting the hippest images, immersed ourselves in the latest trends of that moment and in that specific branch in order to develop the requested promotional material. We quickly discovered, however, that although our client had agreed to everything, they were totally unable to live up to that innovative image. Nor were they at all perceived as such, neither by the market nor by the distributors.

INTERNAL BRANDING

We've already touched upon this briefly: in addition to the importance of disseminating the identity and the emotional values externally, it is also important to keep this alive internally. Internal branding is rather different in principle for employees in retail than for those in manufacturing companies. In the latter, employees are far removed from the relationship between their company's product and the end-user. They usually work in large office buildings in anonymous rooms at rows of computers or at machines in large factory halls. Emotionally, they could just as well be working for another company.

On the retail floor, employees come into direct contact with consumers and are closely involved with the product they sell. Even with big retailers, where many of the staff have an office function, there is a direct relation to what the company does and to the product the company offers, because customer response is measured daily through the cash register. Consequently this large group of people who are physically far removed from the retail floor still have a lot of feeling for the market, for the role of their company and for the role that they themselves play in the whole.

This doesn't take away the importance of internal branding in retail organizations though. Store personnel play an important role in conveying brand values, because they communicate very closely with customers on a one-to-one basis. Internal branding makes employees proud of 'their' company and gives them the feeling of really belonging. It stimulates them to actively and unequivocally express company values in their daily work. And that's important, for the contact between personnel and customer is a moment of truth. The promises that the brand propagates externally through its store image and through all possible means of communication (instore, outstore, mass media) must to a large extent be made good during the contact between customers and personnel.

It's no longer just about intriguing and binding. Your brand presence must also be internally expressed. If your personnel don't live and breathe the brand, how can you ever expect customers to pick up on it? *Erik Saelens (managing director of Brandhome.com)*

It can happen, for instance, that an organization comes out with a strong external brand image, like the example of the store in the photo, with 'So Hip It Hurts' plastered in large letters on its front. But when the store doesn't look hip inside at all and when the salespeople also appear boring and uninteresting, then the promise made 'outside' is not fulfilled 'inside'.

So Hip It Hurts

KAPFERER

As mentioned earlier, the starting point for the development of a company is its identity. It has been shown that identity, and identity stretch in particular, is often difficult to ascertain. What this comes down to is a sort of digging for emotional values, in order to bypass all the rational characteristics. Often it helps to bring employees together from different levels of the company. Various kinds of input produce a broad and complete picture. But on the other hand, identity is not a kind of largest common denominator or a compromise between differing opinions either. Distilling the proper corporate values from all the different views requires a diplomatic approach.

Jean-Noël Kapferer's identity prism is a handy instrument for formulating company identity. The characteristic thing about Kapferer's approach is that he places the company behind the brand (the producer or retail organization) in the central position, and not the brand image or the consumers/target groups that the brand attracts. Which is comparable with the picture sketched in the Retailformula®.

The identity of the organization is discovered by specifying the meaning, intention, and aspirations and mission of the (retail) brand. For when you want to conjure up an image in the world of your customer, first you must make a detailed investigation of what must be depicted and after that, of what must be communicated. To read more about Kapferer's identity prism, please refer to the section on the next page.

As has been said before, identity is not rigid. While investigating and formulating its identity, a company also checks out the possibilities for stretching that identity. Furthermore, a strong identity alone will never be enough to make a retail formula successful. The strength comes from an interplay between the rational and emotional values, for without a well considered range of products you are not a retailer, naturally.

Character cannot be communicated proactively. Nobody can tell his character… we must witness it ourselves to be convinced. Assessing someone else's character is based on personal observation.

Jacques Chevron (founding partner of JRC&A)

JEAN-NOËL KAPFERER ON IDENTITY
(an internationally recognized authority on brands and brand management) from: Strategisch Merkmanagement (Strategic Brand Management), 1995

Kapferer's model deals with six aspects, represented by a prism, that determine brand identity. By filling in each of these aspects, the identity of the brand or organization can be described in relation to its customers and environment. If these aspects are well communicated to the consumer, a strong brand can be created. In that case the brand identity will be transformed within the consumer's world into his or her personal brand image. The following six aspects are distinguished:

1. Physique
A brand has a physique: a combination of prominent independent characteristics that directly come to mind when people think of the brand. It is the foundation of the brand.

2. Personality
A brand has personality, acquires a character. This personalization of the (retail) brand makes it possible to impart deeper meaning to it.

3. Culture
An organization has its own culture. The store (or the product, in the case of a product brand) is the physical embodiment and conveyor of this culture. Culture implies a system of values, a source of inspiration and brand energy.

4. Relation

(Retail) brands enable an immaterial exchange be tween people. Consumers have personal relations with brands, which can differ according to the identity of both.

5. Reflected Customer

A brand reflects the image of a customer. What the brand reflects does not match the target group per se, but it is the image of the target group that the (retail) brand presents to the public.

6. Customer-Self Concept

Customer self-concept is the mirror that the target group holds up to itself. The consumer's attitude toward certain (retail) brands and preference for specific brands helps determine who he/she is as a person. The self-concept reflects what the consumer wants to achieve by choosing the brand.

These six aspects define the brand and enable it to make its identity known. For consumers can decide upon a brand only when they are given the opportunity to find an identity that fits them. The figure shows the division and layout of the prism.

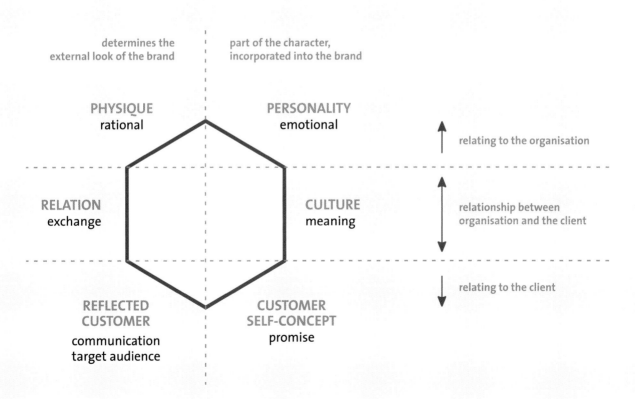

KAPFERER'S IDENTITY PRISM

04
Retail
Branding

WHO CONNECTS TO THE CONSUMER

A store environment is the ideal medium for communicating the values of a retail brand with great precision. The consumer can see, experience, touch, and smell it; he has chosen to be there at that moment and is therefore highly receptive to it. Which is very different than watching a remote commercial in your own cluttered living room.

A LOVE/HATE RELATIONSHIP

The rational aspects of brands are obvious. A brand functions as a guide – it makes a product recognizable. This makes life easier and saves time. Most choices for specific brands are repeatedly made out of habit, certainly when it comes to buying fast-moving goods. Just think of it, a visit to the super-market would otherwise take hours!

With clothing, it works a little bit differently. People in all likelihood will have a few favourites, special brands and stores that they look at first. And even with buying a refrigerator, people will let themselves be guided by the brands they know. The refrigerator has to work well and be roomy enough; a brand that they know is something to go on in the midst of the assortment that they have to choose from. People buy a brand that they've had before (if they've had a good experience with it, at least) or they buy on the recommendation of friends or the salesperson, or after studying brochures and a consumer guide. But alongside this rational approach toward choosing ('refrigerator has to work'), the emotional aspect is already beginning to play quite a role. For whose judgement are you going to rely on and which judgement do you trust the most?

Another mainly rational aspect of a brand is the origin and quality of the product – as the story about the branded cows made clear in the first chapter. The farmer who let his cows graze in the juiciest pastures and gave them a good life gained a name for producing the tastiest steaks. Closer to this era, the Fair Trade stores are an example of a corporation that expressly emphasizes the origin of its products in order to show that they are 'gen-

Fair Trade Shop in Amsterdam (NL)

uine', and have been obtained 'fairly'. The origin of most fast-moving goods is almost impossible to trace, but that makes a brandname all the more a stamp of quality, a guarantee of consistency and excellence.

The emotional characteristics of brands are lot more complex. Many people have a love/hate relationship with brands. Brands are fun, exciting, different, innovative, provide self assurance, and give you status or make you part of a group. Besides this, however, brands can often be rather shady: production methods that just won't do, the enormous amounts of money that circulate in a particular industry and that can be demanded for the products, the arrogance of certain brands, whose companies think they can do anything they want. The social behaviour of corporations is increasingly playing a greater role, a consequence of the fact that industry has become so transparent. We shall have to see whether companies will still be able to ignore 'socially conscious enterprising' a few years from now. For soon increasingly vocal consumers will no longer simply accept all of that. Only, the painful reality is that while a consumer naturally does not want a mosquito curtain to be knotted together by the tiny hands of children in Thailand, she also is not prepared to spend double the money for it.

Maybe that's why people are frequently quick to say in discussions that brands are not important to them or that they dislike brands. And yet people are often guided by brands; if not consciously, then often unconsciously.

Perhaps what also comes into play here is that a sympathetic brand like the Bodyshop is felt to be less like a 'brand'. Similar to when you always do your shopping at an organic food store because you do not like the consumer society and its production methods: it remains a statement, it's who you are and it's your brand, because it is the norm within your group.

True free thought, absolute nonconformity, is rare (and almost impossible). In a certain sense you could say that it is only the province of the poor, who really have no other choice, and the extremely wealthy, who have reached a level where nothing makes a difference anymore. The huge middle classes want to underscore their self-respect and social level by the brands they use or the stores they shop at. As Roland van Kralingen said at a conference on consumer trends, "As soon as consumers reach the next step on the proverbial social ladder, they immediately adjust their patterns of consumption in order to show others on that step that they have arrived through the brands that they buy."

Social climbing is one of the most important reasons why brands still exist.

Roland van Kralingen (marketing and brand strategist)

RETAIL BRANDING VERSUS PRODUCT BRANDING

A great difference between product branding and retail branding is that in many cases products have an anonymous or even fictitious dispatcher, whereas with retail, consumers come in direct contact with the company and/or product.

A Mars chocolate bar, for example, is a product made according to a set recipe in a factory that is not open to the public. The other way round, the people who work there never come in contact with the end-users, because the retail channel lies in between. And those who actually do sell the 'Mars' product to the end-users (the retailers) do not have very much to do with it by virtue of their function. Therefore it is possible to conceive a brand identity for the product, establish it for a specific target group and then fix it in the minds of consumers. Compare the identities of 'Mars', 'M&Ms' and 'Bounty': all very different, yet they come from the same manufacturer (Mars).

Contrast this with a store like Wal-Mart, for example: because of its direct contact with the end-

You can sell a product or service by making it seem better than it is, but not a company. *Gijs ten Kate (strategic partner INC~21)*

user, it must effectively live up to its brand reputation in every aspect, every day. The following will clarify why it is impossible for retailers to escape this.

In a store, the entire retail organization is revealed and the true nature of a company can be experienced. A store, you might say, is the container that holds the entire formula. All the elements of the formula (including the marketing Ps) come together here. The formula should be deliberately filled in from the standpoint of identity, or in other words the 'brand' of the retail organization, with mutual atunement of the elements being important. The picture given by the model provides insight into this.

⊕ PLATFORM DEVELOPMENT®

formula concept / ambition

The model shows that the brand, with its rational and emotional characteristics, is at the core. The components surrounding the core are the operational characteristics – or the formula elements just mentioned – which should be filled in evenly in accordance with the central brand values.

The most important insight that the diagram provides is that a holistic approach toward all elements is essential. All elements taken together form the brand experience as is felt by the customer. The customer is a true expert in the area of understanding signs and behaviour and knows how to appraise their worth too. When an element is underexposed or improperly filled in, a customer notices that something doesn't quite add up or is out of whack. Maybe he can't immediately put his finder on it, but he will thoroughly feel it as such. In chapter 7 we will discuss the Platform Development® model in detail.

ADVANTAGES OF RETAIL BRANDING
Retail brands have gained in popularity in the past few years. And they indeed have a number of advantages above product brands. In the first place, they are closer to the consumer. The physical store space offers the possibility of literally and figuratively communicating with consumers at the moment of purchase (one-to-one marketing). Retailers can show who they are and what they stand for through the store formula. Moreover, in principle retailers are neutral, because the

choice of product brand (or store brand, if present) is left to the consumers. Retailers help consumers because they have the possibility of making a shrewd preselection and presenting this in a surveyable manner (in *their* specific manner, that is).

Once a consumer knows and trusts a retailer and has good memories about a store, the foundation has been laid for a long-lasting relationship that will (hopefully) ultimately lead to customer loyalty.

PRODUCERS WHO GO INTO RETAIL

Is this the reason why producers of brands begin their own stores? Most likely, for this is an ideal way to show what the brand stands for, and it offers an ideal platform for developing alternative activities in extension of the brand. In the Netherlands, the Bertolli olive oil brand has opened a 'Tuscany Lunch Café'. They feature Italian wines, Italian sandwiches and salads – and naturally they sell olive oil there. All of this can also be ordered through the Internet, by fax or telephone. The concept is very successful: Bertolli sandwiches are now even sold at petrol stations! The Bertolli olive oil brand has very little to do with the *foccacias* lying in the coolers at petrol stations. But it is extremely cleverly done: Bertolli proves to be such a strong and credible brand that this broadening of its product line has been completely accepted by consumers.

Retail branding creates brand preference, which goes beyond the product or service in itself.

Unilever's Bertolli Lunch café in The Hague (NL)

HOW TO CONNECT WITH THE CONSUMER

Connecting with the consumer means thinking from the consumer's point of view. When we talk with clients about the competition in the markets in which they operate, they tend to name direct, similar or adjacent players in the field. They don't look for threats too far away, and certainly not at the brand level. The following example will shed a clear light upon this.

Elle is a renowned fashion magazine, which early on expanded from fashion into lifestyle and human interest. Next came separate publications about living, dining, and gardening. And a website offering information but also products. After that came a store, a fashion store to be sure, but that's where their beginnings lie, after all. Meanwhile, what with fashion, lifestyle, living, dining and gardening, it is not inconceivable that the following step will be a complete department store. For customers *Elle* is their guide in the world. People will say, "I'm an *Elle* kind of person." *Elle* is the binding factor that selects, inspires, indicates and innovates. We are not saying, however, that the *Elle* store is also a successful concept, because we don't know exactly what the quality of the store is or whether it has had any success at all. This of course has to do with the principle that heavy competition can come from unexpected quarters. From that starting point, and within this context, we have created our definition of a brand: a brand is a platform, a meeting point for kindred spirits.

The world of Elle is constantly growing larger

Elle shop in Bluewater (Kent)

A brand is a platform, a meeting point for kindred spirits.

Kindred spirits, but not necessarily equal, for you can very well be a fan of a brand and simultaneously feel that it is out of your league. The kindredness is in the subtle weighing of what the brand offers and what customers are searching for or desire. The kindred feeling also surfaces in encounters between customers who recognize each other's shared traits in relation to the brand experience – or pick up static, because somebody who doesn't fit the bill is sporting 'your' brand. From the standpoint of the brand, this has got to do with clear choices in terms of the values, tone of voice and look & feel that are part of the identity.

Take a look at the photograph of the EDC show window in this regard. Esprit has supplemented its regular line of products, a basic clothing style, with a clothing label and instore formula named EDC (Esprit de Corps, the official company name). With this collection they display an obviously selective image: "If you're the sort of person who is in these photos, you'll find it here." But also, "If not, you'll have to go someplace else."

Terence Conran, a major English entrepreneur, designer and stylist, works from the opposite principle: he wants to attract as many people as possible. In his own words, "I'm simply convinced that when you offer right-minded, intelligent people something that's well-made, well-designed, of good quality and for an affordable price, they'll like it and buy it.

In addition to having his own design agency, he founded the Habitat company in 1964 in an attempt to sell a different sort of lifestyle to the English in a new and inspiring way. Later came the Conran Shops (upgraded Habitats), which he expanded to other continents, and threw himself into the development of large restaurants and food stores. Throughout his entire career he has written books about dwellings and living and continued to design and style many products.

'Esprit de Corps': a line of clothing that is younger and more selective than that of Esprit.

In the former garage of the speed record car 'the Bluebird' on King's Road in London he realized a largescale project likewise named Bluebird. It consists of a forecourt with a flower stall, a brasserie/coffeeshop, several bars, a dining club, a gastronomic supermarket, run by Sainsbury nowadays, a small Conran Shop and a large restaurant on the first floor. Conran certainly knows how to tempt people, because they willingly queue up for a seat in the restaurant. For Saturday afternoon lunches too, for which they easily spend around 50 euros per person! And Conran also knows how to project a total concept – the physical evidence of branding is apparent everywhere in the Conran Shop. On the wall hangs a photo of Sir Terence in bed, in a bathrobe, with his own china and a cigar. And when you're there on a Saturday afternoon, you're buying a bit of his success. And you secretly think that if you purchase a tea set or bathrobe like his, on Sunday morning you'll be sitting just as comfortably in your own lavish bed. In reality you'll be up at 8:00 because you have to take the kids to football and your bedroom doesn't look at all that extravagant, but for one moment, just one moment, you're Conran.

Conran's Bluebird gastrodrome

A relationship is created when a retail space ceases to be merely a merchandising outlet and instead becomes a place where a passion is shared. *Jean-Noël Kapferer*

*Sephora flagship on the
Champs-Élysées, Paris*

Sephora Blanc in Bercy

Another example is Sephora, a chain of cosmetic stores that sells large brands in addition to non-branded products of its own (soap, lipstick and the like). They sell well-known brands from couturiers like Armani, Chanel and Dolce & Gabbana, but in such a convincing manner that instead of buying Armani or Chanel, you're buying Armani or Chanel *from Sephora*. Their presentation, their service, the clothing their staff wears, their packaging and the authority of their knowledge and assortment are so convincing and overwhelming that this brand surpasses the strongest of product brands. Here the power of producers is, in a manner of speaking, steamrollered right over. And that's what retail branding indeed is – an umbrella, whereby the product brands that the store carries are subordinate to its retail brand, or at any event can be measured against it.

And just like leaders are expected to do, Sephora is moving on. The fact of the matter is, market leaders are often imitated; looking ahead and develop-ing new directions is more essential than trying to prevent imitation. In 2001 Sephora set up a new, all-white store in Bercy: Sephora Blanc. The concept revolves around well-being. The product range includes esoteric oils, incense, massage products, etc. It is a spiritual, introverted shop, very different from the company's extroverted shops that are all about exterior aspects and seduction.

Brands that succeed think and behave like challengers – even if they are leaders in their category.

Stuart Burnett (creative director of Perspectives Red Cell)

A third example is Armani's flagship store in Milan – where Armani's clothing and perfumes can be found, naturally, but also its interior decorating collection, books, a coffee shop, a restaurant, a floor with Sony products, flowers and since recently, its own bonbons. The flowers, in fact, are a marvellous example of what clever branding is all about. Surely you can picture the following situation vividly: a woman visits her friend's home and says, "What beautiful tulips!" To which the friend can proudly respond, "Yes, aren't they. From Armani." That's when you know you have a very strong brand.

Armani flagship in Milaan

In addition to being an interesting form of co-branding, the department that features Sony products also serves another goal. In this department you can play computer games, watch mega-widescreen TV, try out the newest products; in short, a paradise and a hangout (see photo) for kids who don't yet have the money to buy such things themselves. But they come just the same and have a positive experience. Armani will be pleasantly engraved in their memories. In this manner, Armani subtly generates goodwill with the younger generation. And when that generation is old enough and has the money, they will come back – and hopefully buy.

The Sony department in the Armani flagship

These examples of successful retailers make it clear that more than one positioning is possible, and that everyone does things in their own way. Success depends upon a number of factors. We see that Conran expresses a certain kind of lifestyle. He links products with his own name. But besides that he sells lots of brand products, brands he picks out because they fit with his taste. The 'Conran figure' plays an important role in that positioning.

Sephora sells very many different brands, but also carries products under its own label. Unlike Conran, Sephora is a real store brand, but it does have a strong identity that is revealed in different capacities. Sephora is innovative, is developing the market of perfume and personal care, and it has style.

Although Armani originally was Armani himself, the 'Armani figure' does not really play a role in the store. All products are of course sold under the Armani brandname. Although Armani's flagship is an exception, his more 'ordinary' stores are aimed at the upper class. The stores are fairly exclusive, not just everybody walks inside (or dares to!). The character of the stores is accordingly somewhat aloof and sophisticated.

For a formula to be a success, it doesn't make any difference whether retailers sell just their own brand, just the brands of producers, or a combination of both. It also doesn't make any difference whether retailers are at the high end of the market or discounters. What counts is that retailers make a clear-cut choice and aim for a matching brand experience.

The paradigm shift is that the shop will have to sell its aura rather than merely its products.

Stephen Anderson (retail designer at BDP)

RETAIL BRAND ARCHETYPES
In the following table we have attempted to give an overview of possible forms of Retail Branding. It is a mix of positioning combined with character traits and brand values and the manner in which a retailer does business. Yet this categorization does not do justice to the original and at times complex character of the wide diversity of retail brands. After all, a person would also prefer not be pigeonholed. The categories therefore must not be interpreted as a sort of 'list' from which you can simply choose a 'brand character'. Moreover, it will often be possible to place stores in more than one category (although frequently there will be one category in which they will excel). It could also turn out that this blueprint is incomplete; after all, retail is always undergoing development. Consider this a guideline, and in some cases an eye opener, for sometimes discounters can be very strong Retail Brands too.

The effect of branding is that a whole world opens up when you see, experience or even think of the brand.

TYPE	OPTIONS	EXPLENATION	RETAIL EXAMPLES
Personification	private selections	entrepreneurs; the shop reflects the character of the person	Paul Smith, (Conran shops)
	the person is the brand	the founder of the company plays an important role	Donna Karan, Conran, Tommy Hilfiger
	an imaginary person is the brand	a fictitious person is presented as frontperson	Colette
Socially Responsible Entrepreneurship	environment oriented	SRE from an environmental and ideological standpoint	Bodyshop
	critical of the social structure	social issues/facts exposed/shown in different light	Benneton, (Camper)
Discount	super discount	it's only about price	One dollar shop (several food and clothes stores)
	stylish	price important, but added value through the manifestation of wilfulness and style	Muji, Hema, outlet centres with a theme
Innovative	very specific and unique	the unique, experimental design of the store plays a very important role in the proposition	Comme des Garçons, Prada, Mandarina Duck
	market leader	a forerunner in terms of new developments	Camper, Ikea, (Sephora)
Authenticity	traditional, nostalgic	old values/times revived, or freshly transformed into the spirit of the times	Burberry, Mont Blanc, De Bonneterie
	sincere, reliable	mostly services, where it's important that the consumer trust you	banks, energy suppliers, insurance companies
Sophistication (highbrow)	upper class	in a rather aloof manner	Gucci, Armani, Prada
	the store as a stage	the store is a showroom	Marni, New Prada stores
	smooth	in a more open/transparent manner	Miu Miu, Dunhill, (Armani flagship in Milan)
Sensory Retailing	experience	the experience is very explicit	Nike Town, Disney Store, American Girl Place
	in style	an experience on a more implicit, emotional or spiritual level	5 Senses, Rituals, Lush, Sephora, Cosmetic Garden
Ruggedness	tough, outdoorsy	adventurous, challenging	R.E.I., Decathlon, most sports and outdoor stores
	manly	sturdy, handyman	D.I.Y. stores, brown and white goods stores
Fashionable	up-to-date	stores that do well, focusing on a specific group through their presentation and assortment	Mango, Zara, Gap, etc.
	trendy, hip	stores that do well, focusing on trendsetters through their presentation and assortment	Diesel, Chill Out in Bijenkorf, Fish and Chips (in Antwerp)
Abundance	literally	the product does the job, large volumes	Uniqlo, Dean & DeLuca
	figuratively	the product plays a part in creating the atmosphere	Ikea, Barnes & Noble

5

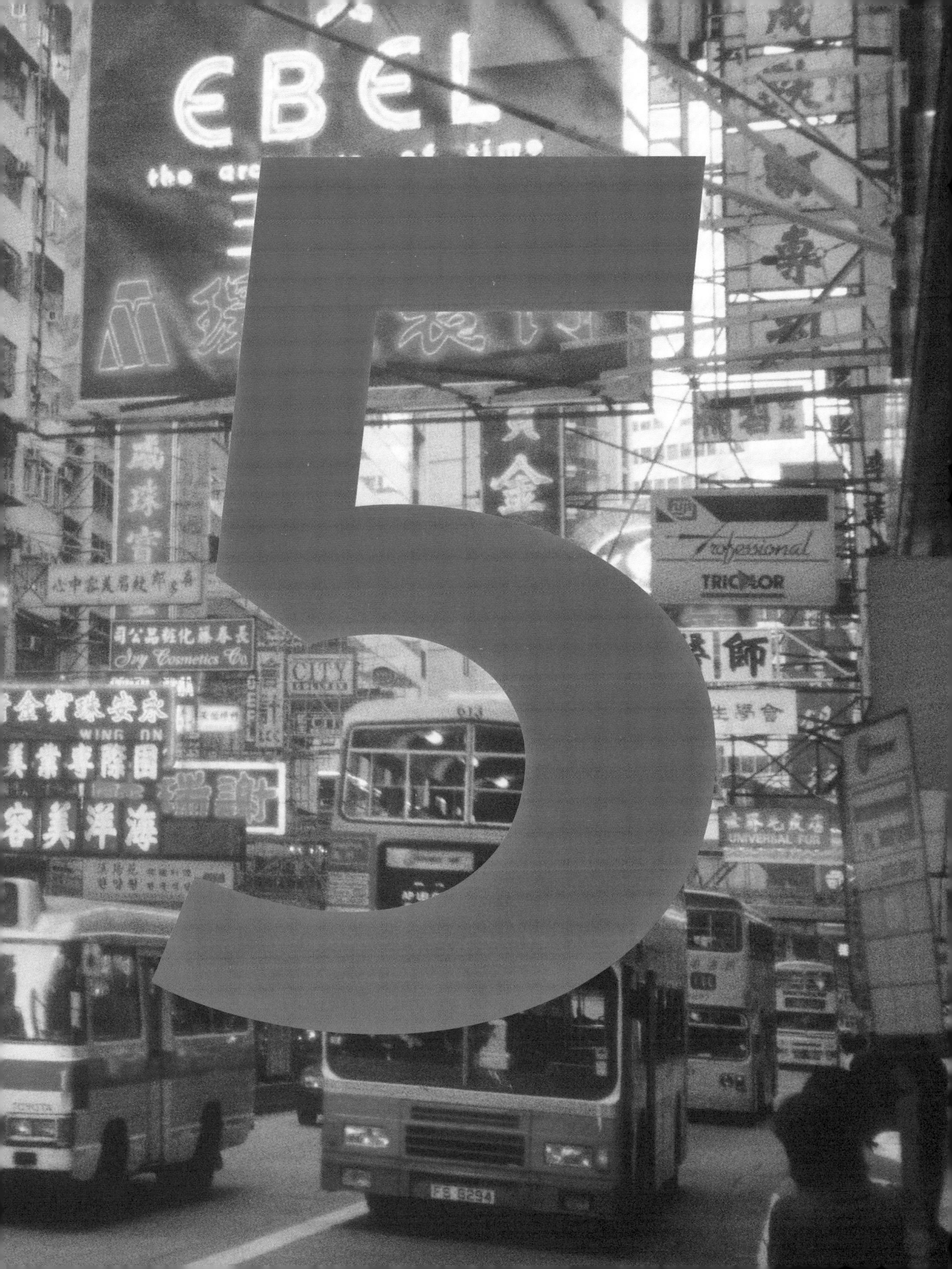

05
Hong Kong Street

The best products in the finest shopping environment and the friendliest sales clerks in the world are not enough to draw consumers into a store. For after all, none of that can be seen from the outside. The consumer must first be willing to focus his attention on the store, otherwise he will never even notice it.

DRAWING ATTENTION

The store can attract that attention by being distinctive and sending out the proper signals. But how does it work and how do you achieve this?

To gain more insight into how that works, it is useful to take an objective look at store formulas. As this is rather difficult to do in your own country, let alone in your own city, we'll examine an arbitrary shopping street in Hong Kong. Imagine a familiar store formula (your own, for instance, or otherwise a local store formula) in this street. What would that signboard and that logo signify? Just what is it that would make the people standing at the beginning of this street say, "I'd like to take a look in there sometime, that seems interesting (or trendy, or just my style)"?

A street in HongKong.
What are all those signboards
trying to say?

The whole day long our senses are flooded with all sorts of different impressions. The way to keep a grip on the chaos surrounding us is to pigeonhole as much as possible in order to gain an overview.

van der Lubbe and van Zoest (semoticians)

SIGNS AND SEMIOTICS

Throughout the day, we are confronted by countless signs. Fortunately, humans are able to unerringly interpret all of these signs. Signs help us make decisions, ensuring that we don't have to think too long about those decisions. This has to do with semiotics, the study of signs, a science which analyzes how signs as elements of communication are interpreted. Although people approach signs subjectively, various types of signs elicit universally similar experiences. Some are consciously memorized, such as traffic signals, others are learned collectively, for example, that a diamond is valuable. Well-known logos and brand names are also signs, of course. Their meaning is familiar to us: we are aware that Nike stands for sports clothing and sport shoes or that Boots is a drugstore. We amplify that rational information with personal experiences, opinions and preferences. Such emotional information is what most determines whether we choose a brand or not. But unknown brand names will be purely and objectively interpreted and judged.

Various brand names can be seen on the signboards hanging in the Hong Kong shopping street. MaxMara and Mitsubishi (brands that are recognizable) will evoke both rational and emotional associations. But there are also unknown word pictures and symbols that perhaps are brands: In the middle of the photograph there is a black signboard with yellow lettering showing the words 'Just Gold' next to several Chinese characters. And although I took this photo myself, I can no longer remember exactly what kind of store it was. My intuitive feeling is that that the sign does not stand for a luxury jeweller with just one wristwatch displayed in the window for $25,000 but rather for a store with big bins full of gold jewellery bearing the sign 'Buy More for Less'. That's just one possible association, naturally. Perhaps someone else would interpret the golden letters on the black background as chic, because gold on black fits within that idiom. By definition, neither is incorrect. The interpretation of signs is dependant on personal and cultural factors. You therefore will have to give a lot of consideration to how you deal with your signs (logos) and think about what associations the store must evoke and what style it should project.

EXPECTATION MANAGEMENT

Further down the street there's another familiar symbol: yellow arches on a red background. Those yellow arches have indoctrinated, conditioned and Pavlovian-ized us for years. With the yellow arches, you as a consumer know what it looks like inside,

how it smells, what's on the menu, how the service and waiting times run, what the price is and the taste is and even what guilt feelings you will have after you have yet again eaten another one of those hamburgers.

The pursuit of this policy worldwide in accordance with the principle of operational excellence creates an expectancy that is fulfilled every time. Good implementation and staying faithful to expectations and to the promise that has been created or taught is optimal 'expectation management'. It is one of the crucial components of a successful retail formula. It does not, for that matter, have to proceed from the principle of operational excellence, but can also be realized through 'customer intimacy' or 'product leadership'. The characteristics of these three principles are listed here in brief (source: &Samhoud, Service Management Magazine 1, January 2000).

Operational Excellence:
MacDonald's, Ikea
·   predictability of the offer
·   dependability and ease of service
·   optimalization of the price/quality relationship
·   customer and process oriented organizations

Customer Intimacy:
Chiefly service-related companies: banks, hotels, energy suppliers
·   anticipating specific and changing wishes of clients
·   the best total solution (based on 'solving the problem of the client' instead of 'delivering products or services')

- high level of personal service > value added to products/services
- always keep surprising customers (customer delight)
- loyalty and lifetime value

Product Leadership:
Sephora, Disney, mainly product brands
- creating and launching superior new products
- quality, design and functionality all play an important role
- constantly keep innovating

It goes without saying that the promise that the enterprise creates and fulfils will have to perfectly match the needs of the customer. This immediately reveals the vulnerability of an enterprise, for it takes work to fulfil promises and to make consumers realize that the product or service will bring them all sorts of advantages or improvements of quality. On top of that, it's often a question of 'balancing on the edge of a precipice': In some cases, one bad experience with the brand is enough for a consumer to reject you for a long time, or even for good.

When an enterprise is temporarily unable to meet expectations for one reason or another, it is important to manage the situation and to actively or proactively approach, warn and compensate customers. This prevents disappointment and, what's more, can sometimes lead to extra-positive reactions.

"Dear customers, a vendor shipping discrepancy has resulted in certain out of stocks on various D.L. Jardines products. Please excuse the inconvenience! Thank you."

An important medium for transmitting messages and closing sales is now the store and the aisle. That building, that place, has become a great big three-dimensional advertisement for itself. Signage, shelf position, display space and special fixtures all make it either likelier or less likely that a shopper will buy a particular item (or any item at all). *Paco Underhill*

THE PROCESS OF CHOOSING A STORE

In an unfamiliar shopping street with many unfamiliar signs, the process of choosing a store is largely based on unbiased interpretations. In our own shopping street where most of the signs and stores are familiar, our interpretations are more based on the knowledge that we already have.

In most cases, the process of choosing a store begins at home. When people are planning to go shopping, they have a picture of a real or fictitious shopping street in mind. And they imagine which stores they will visit, in what order. If shopping has to be done out of necessity, more rational considerations determine which stores appear on a person's mental shortlist. Location is an important consideration here, but also, for instance: "Can I park my car in the area?" "If I go to that particular store now, I can get everything I need (= save time)." "That's where they've got the best selection at the right price." And so forth. With shopping purely for pleasure, people also think in advance about which shops they definitely want to visit, out of familiarity and habit, as a reinforcement of self-esteem, because of hedonistic factors, or for whatever other reason.

In brief, the shortlist that people create in their minds largely determines which stores they will ultimately visit. The fact that people are able to choose a store while still at home, is due to the identity of the store, its personality and brand value. Choosing takes place in the first instance through the senses: seeing, hearing, smelling, tasting, touching. On the basis of this, people make personal choices. And that's why the physical manifestation of a store as translated through the various senses is so important. For this is how we can recollect those stores and summon up past experiences in our minds. A store that plays heavily on all the senses is Lush. Probably you can already see the handwritten signs, the colours, the little jars, appearing before your mind's eye right now, and naturally the presentation of the big 'cakes' of soap, as well as all those scents that always pervade the stores – provided that you are acquainted with the store, obviously.

Lush: a pleasure for the senses

Let's take a little test: Where do you go to buy a singing teakettle?

- We don't know many brands. Only in the top segment perhaps.

Which stores come to mind?

- Crate & Barrel?
- A local shop on the corner?
- Ikea, Carrefour, Williams Sonoma or your favourite department store?
- Or do you visit the market first?
- Or do you look at all the stores?
  And a pair of Levi's jeans, where do you buy them? And where do you buy a suit?

What it all comes down to is 'knowing', 'looking', 'buying'. If consumers don't know your store, then they won't come. And if they don't come, they certainly won't buy. Occupying a place in the memories of consumers – a top-of-mind position – is extremely valuable.

RETAIL CHOICE DIAGRAM®

It's not easy to reach number one in the minds of consumers, to be there and stay there. Furthermore, unexpected situations can easily upset intended routes: another store suddenly attracts their attention, whining kids want to go home, a sale prompts them to make a different choice.

What a retailer can do is see to it that all the steps that a consumer takes are filled in, from the sofa at home to the product on the shelf. The Retail Choice Diagram® demonstrates this.

Filling in all stages of the Retail Choice Diagram® requires both a rational and an emotional approach.

⊕ RETAIL CHOICE DIAGRAM®

On the emotional side, all expressions obviously must project the identity of the store. But these two and three dimensional signs will also pull the customer into the store almost without his being aware of it. After that the signs lead the customer by means of their stratification to the right department and finally to the product that he has come for. The focus is constantly shifted, and the customer is literally guided on his journey through the store in that manner. For only when all levels are filled in does the customer journey have a smooth flow.

On the rational side, the diagram is more of a checklist for the retailer. Are all the steps filled in? Starting with the customer at home (via folders, advertisements and/or the Internet) and then being recognizable in the street (ads, signboards, etc.) and being recognizable through the personal aura of the store (logo, storefront, shop windows and so forth). The store itself will have to 'work' by means of a functional layout with functional communications; and besides that, communications related to the brand personality and products are also desirable. The considerations that are involved in these outstore, around the store and instore communications will be treated in the next chapter, where we'll also be discussing the Retail Choice Diagram® in more detail.

SEMIOTICS

Based on the book Teken en Betekenis (Sign and Meaning) by Jan C.A. van der Lubbe and Aart J.A. van Zoest

All those signs in shopping streets are not there for nothing, of course. They are trying to tell us something: their purpose is to convey information. What's more, information can only be conveyed by means of signs. In order to fully understand the context of this sentence, it is important to take a closer look at the theory of Charles Sanders Peirce (1838-1914), who can be considered the founder of semiotics.

Peirce clarified the process whereby information is transmitted by means of signs with the semiotic triangle, pictured in figure 1.

Figure 1

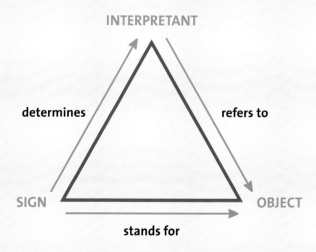

The sign, also called the signifier, indicates the object. The sign is a picture or the name of the object, for example. The sign is what is interpreted; the interpretation refers back to the object. Peirce distinguishes three types of signs:

Icon: resemblance between sign and object: a simple image, outline, illustration, drawing or photo (for instance, most advertising messages)

Index: naturally inevitable or existential relationship between sign and object (footprints indicate someone walked there, fever indicates an infection in the body)

Symbol: arbitrary relationship between sign and object, existing through agreement, regulations or convention (words, concepts, language – the most signifiers in human society by far)

The signifier is always abstract and always perceptible. Thus by definition the signifier can always be materialized in one way or another. In contrast, the object (also described as 'that which the sign refers to') need not be perceptible. You can talk about a table without having to see it. The word table is perceptible, however, because it is spoken. Sometimes the object can't even be visible; for example, a concept that is indicated by a gesture (the signifier): the 'waggling your hand beside your head' sign stands for the concept of 'delicious'.

Signs are perceptible, but this ultimately comes down to the interpretant, for the interpretant is the meaning that the sign evokes. The aim during communication is for the meaning to come across exactly as intended; otherwise there is a question of incomprehension and miscommunication. During 'ordinary' verbal conversations most misunderstandings can be cleared up fairly easily, but getting your message across in a shopping street with images and perhaps a few words is already a good deal more difficult.

Let's take a semiotic look at the example of the 'Just Gold' signboard. The signifier (an icon) is the signboard itself: gold letters on a black background. We cannot read the Chinese characters; perhaps they can be interpreted as icons for the Chinese society. The fact that we can read the words 'Just Gold' is based on an agreement (unless, of course, we don't happen to speak English): we understand the letters and the words that they make and that's why they initially function as a symbol. But the graceful design of the letters and the colour have an iconic function as well. They say something about the style and nature of the store.

The store (formula) is the object. On the one hand it is a tangible object: we see the store, the products, the pricing, the personnel. On the other hand it is intangible: we have certain feelings about the logo, the presentation and the tone & style of the store. For most people perceive the visual merchandising, the instore communications and the design (and layout) of the store unconsciously. The signboard (the signifier) stands for the store formula (the object) and attempts to make all of this clear (see figure 2).

Whether or not the signifier actually comes across as intended becomes clear when you can learn more about the interpretant, the meaning people attribute

Figure 2

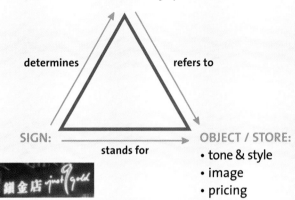

to it and the associations people have upon seeing it. It is, of course, desirable that consumers understand precisely what kind of store is behind that signboard. "But interpretants cannot be directly transmitted; the only thing that we can hope after the transference of signs is that the other will have the same semiotic triangle in his head as we do," says Jan van der Lubbe in *Teken en Betekenis*.

All that can be done about this is to try to depict the signifier (or actually, signifiers) as clearly and unambiguously as possible. Repetition or redundancy can help in this regard. When a store disseminates signifiers that evoke the same associations in all of its expressions (logo, house style, store exterior and interior, range of products, mass media expressions, instore communications, and so forth) then it is more likely that the result will be the 'correct' interpretation.

Besides their purely visual image, the meaning of the words 'Just Gold' also plays an important part when we attempt to picture the store. The word 'just' can be interpreted in several ways. But this is the domain of 'semantics' and to discuss that in detail here would be going too far.

Because everybody knows McDonald's, a few other factors come into play in the interpretation of the yellow arches. More meanings are attributed to the yellow arches than simply associations with the fast food restaurant itself. People can have both positive and negative associations with the yellow arches, which are different for every individual. For instance: Big Mac, a tasty treat, eating out with the kids (happy meal), you get what you expect, freedom and Americanization. But also: greasy and tasteless food, the consumer society, exploitation of employees and Third World countries.

All sorts of associations are possible because in a manner of speaking the triangle has already been circumnavigated several times. For in fact the triangle is a circular process. Not only have we been confronted with the yellow arches on the restaurant's signboard, but we've also seen them on television, at festivals and we've read about them in newspapers and critical books and magazines. So our associations are fine-tuned, as it were. (Peirce calls this process 'semiosis'.)

06

Instore Communi-cation

ASK ATTENTION, GET ATTENTION, GIVE ATTENTION

The task of stores has changed from being a place where products could be obtained through personalized service to a storehouse where customers themselves pick their products. The consequences of this are enormous.

FROM FULL-SERVICE TO SELF-SERVICE

Ever since the late 1950s and early 1960s, personal contact between retailers and customers has tapered off sharply with the rise of all sorts of self-service in Europe. Well that's obvious, you'll say, and inherent to the word self-service, but the observation goes deeper than that. The issue raised is this: Was self-service a logical consequence of consumers becoming more individualistic and more speed oriented? Or did retail take the lead in adopting this development from the United States? After all, it showed up earlier there, and the United States was the great example for Europe after the second world war. This cannot be established with certainty, but the consequences of the disappearance of personal contact are enormous. Producers fairly soon got wise to the fact that they had to make themselves heard – they had to become branded – in order to stick in the minds of consumers. With retailers, this realization has actually only really sunk in during the last few years. For the distance between consumers and retailers has also widened because of the increased scale that is the result of self-service. This makes branding necessary for retailers too, for otherwise anonymity can easily rear its ugly head.

Self-service can be considered a real innovation because of the major changes it has introduced in the retail landscape. Just think, for example of the enormous development of all sorts of logistic processes, which is still going on. Yet from the customer's viewpoint very little perceptible progress has been made after that initial step. To put it another way, in this area there still are tremendous possibilities in terms of the interpretation of a self-service concept!

Although self-service ties in well with our changed and changing society, fastpaced life and greatly increased individualization, it is often experienced as a decrease in quality. Your own shopkeeper with his personal approach has disappeared and been replaced by store personnel with a lack of knowledge about things and a lack of interest. But then again, a degree of subtlety is warranted here – often it's also the customers who adopt a less than inspiring attitude. Their interaction with the personnel should not be underestimated.

PERSONNEL

The role of personnel has also been transformed as a result of self-service. Nowadays their first task is to take care of the shelves, so that the filled shelves can supply the clients – not only in supermarkets, but also, for instance, in department stores and large clothing stores. The helpfulness and status of personnel and the hierarchical manner in which customers used to be treated (customer = king) has disappeared. This is comparable with our transformed society; its rather strong hierarchical construction has given way for the notion that everyone is equal. And that is reflected in the retail trade – the employees do not feel subserviant to the customers. Moreover, people have developed. They are better educated, demand more and expect more from life, whereas in the past people were more resigned to their roles and had no ambitions or expectations of climbing up the social ladder. That's why working in a store nowadays is not inviting enough to be a career, which has resulted in lots of part-time workers and large turnover of staff.

But an awareness of the changed role of employees has often not yet really penetrated with customers. And thus personnel do not meet the expectations that people have of them, which leads to misunderstandings and frustrations. In addition to that, customers are terribly ambivalent. Sometimes they want immediate help and advice (and feel aggrieved if they don't get it without asking), and at other times they want to go their own way (and become annoyed when help is offered them). Fortunately there are still enough personnel around who know how to deal with this – for such customers are not easy.

On the other hand, it does happen to be true that store personnel often no longer have specific knowledge or expertise in the field because it is not necessary for their changed job function. Yet cutomers still have a desire for contact, inspiration and information. And the desire for contact is what the personnel should now be answering. The desire for inspiration and information is sooner answered by the store and its filled shelves. That's also what makes the store so important as a sales machine. After all, the store has to do a good deal of the sales work itself! The essence of instore communications is linked with this. Make sure that the store works – in terms of functionality, but also as a means of directly and indirectly conveying the unique formula identity. Instore communications involve all levels of communication within the store. Besides graphic elements and written communication, that also includes such things as routing, visual merchandising, products and personnel. Instore communications help the customer make relevant choices and are aimed at raising the conversion level and the receipt amount for both the short and mid term.

ELABORATION OF THE RETAIL CHOICE DIAGRAM®

The Retail Choice Diagram®, which has already been touched upon in the last chapter, delineates the path of the customer from 'the sofa at home' to the actual purchase in the store. On one side the model shows what physical steps the customer actually must take in order to buy an arbitrary product. And the other side shows what means a retailer has at his disposal to guide the customer on each step of the path.

First we will examine the Retail Choice Diagram® from the customer's perspective. We already became acquainted with the first step in the last chapter. In brief: a customer will draw up a shortlist of the stores he wants to visit before he leaves home. (A retailer, therefore, must try to get in that top-of-mind position.)

It is the desire for contact that personnel should now be answering. The desire for inspiration and information is sooner answered by the store itself and the filled shelves.

⊕ RETAIL CHOICE DIAGRAM®

HOME	EXTERIOR	STORE	DEPARTMENT	SUB-DEPARTMENT	PRODUCT BRAND
• advertising	• billboard	• signposting	• signposting	• store engineering	• visuals / graphics
• promotions	• signposting	• store brand	• framework	• visual merchandising	• visual merchandising
• clubcard	• signing	• clothing	• atmosphere posters	• atmosphere posters	• packaging
• mailing	• atmosphere		• props	• props	• collection
• brochure			• product	• brand communication	

Let's take a man who wants to buy a suit as an example. He sets out after having decided which store to visit (as the first). It's a large store which offers a wide range of choice and has both a men's and women's department. Once arriving at the proper street, he sees the store from afar. This image should be an extension of the feeling that he had about the store at home. Physically, visually, and even from a distance, the store must live up to that image – and preferably surpass it. Next he stands in front of the store. The windows, the product presentations and the first communication create a direct impression of the atmosphere of the store brand. Upon entering, the actual embrace occurs. The total atmosphere of the retail brand now predominates and the thought that had arisen 'on the sofa at home' is now completely substantiated. He again thinks about what he has come for and figures out where he has to be by the clear-cut difference between the men's and women's departments: a different atmosphere within the same identity. In the men's department he recognizes the brand identity of the casual department on one side and the career department on the other. The latter is more formal than the jeans and T-shirts in the casual section. He walks to the suit department. Gradually the product is now becoming more important than the retailer, for the focus is zooming in. He sees the retailer's label and a number of other brands, let's say Armani, Boss and Breuer. With designer brands, the atmosphere of the brand is more important than the atmosphere of the store and Armani or Boss can add their own entourage to that of the store brand – provided that it is relevant for that place, with that product. He decides

upon a suit, steps back into the atmosphere of the store and perhaps makes a new choice for another product.

Whether buying a suit or a toothbrush, the consumer goes through all of these steps. Between each step in the chain it is up to the retailer to hold onto the red thread and strengthen it, or cut it off and, in a manner of speaking, leave the consumer to his fate.

RETAIL CHOICE DIAGRAM® FROM
THE PERSPECTIVE OF THE RETAILER

The mass-media communications that consumers encounter at home (folders, brochures, advertisements in magazines and newspapers, TV and the Internet, etc.) must be related to what goes on in the store. The retailer asks for attention, gets that attention when the consumer comes to the store and will have to give the customer the attention he wants.

> Ask attention, Get attention, Give attention

'Ask attention' refers to the soliciting advertising methods, a mass-media method of campaigning. These are rational on one hand: weekly specials or the announcement of a new product, for example, with the intention of luring people into the store. On the other hand, they have an emotional nature: the retailer tries to convey his brand character.

'Get attention' stands for the reaction of the customers. They come.

With 'give attention' the action is back with the retailer again. The customer has come, and says:

"You called me, here I am, show me what you've got." This is the 'moment of truth'. In many cases the soliciting advertisement is repeated here once again – with its mass-media tone, whereas a one-to-one tone is desirable here. After all, the instore communications must replace the missing shop-keeper (who understood what his specific customer wanted) through information, personalized sales offerings and presentations rich with ideas. A few years ago a bank conducted an advertising campaign with the payoff, "How much are you really worth?" Meaning: How much money do you have and how much can you borrow on top of that? An approach which works fine in the mass media, but is unsuitable in a one-to-one conversation. It is not part of our behavioral conventions. A translation from mass media to instore would be appropriate here.

Around the store communications are closer to the symbolic idiom and housestyle of the retailer. This includes the architecture of the building, outdoor signposting and oftimes large signs bearing the logo alongside roads leading up to the store. Especially for stores that are located on the outskirts of a town or city, these three elements play an important role. The architectural freedom allowed in this area makes it possible for retailers to express their character through very individual and recognizable buildings. For some retailers this is precisely why they set up business out of town. The symbolic idiom they use is usually very clear, because cars that race past in a few seconds must be able to recognize or identify the retailer. The most familiar examples of this are of course Ikea and McDonald's.

Besides this, around the store communications include such things as the delivery trucks, the out-door sign (illuminated sign), shop windows (with visual merchandising) and posters, all of which may incorporate soliciting messages (that tie in with the brand character in terms of tone, naturally).

Instore communications rest on four pillars (whereby personnel, strictly speaking, are disregarded):
1. Focus on the Formula and the Brand
2. Focus on Function
3. Focus on the Product
4. Focus on Promotion

THE FOUR PILLARS OF INSTORE COMMUNICATIONS

1. Focus on the Formula and the Brand

In other words, all of the literal and figurative expressions that refer to the formula and the brand. A statement by the entrance that makes promises to customers is a literal expression, for example. Although in fact, simply placing it there is an expression of the brand. Moreover, it's clever to have the store name and the logo repeated within the store, the chance is then greater that customers will remember the name, like a virtual fingerprint. After all, you want to stay or become top-of-the mind. In order to convey actual character, however, you will need intangible means. For it is not possible to literally communicate or talk about character; people will have to experience it through all of their senses (think of music, scents, lighting, choice of materials, stimulating the taste buds and so forth). Two-dimensional and three-dimensional elements support the whole, contribute to the atmosphere and the tone & style. With two-dimensional, we're talking about all kinds of graphic means, such as typo graphy, color, pictograms, images (photography, digital and moving) and with three-dimensional, we're refering to elements like design, visual merchandising (volume, lifestyle, product combinations and so forth) and the arrangement, layout and routing of the store, as well as intangibles like fragrance, music and lighting. All of these elements together (multi-sensory experiences) convey the store personality and form the store experience.

The illustrations show several examples of stores that have created a store atmosphere in their own manner.

Three supermarkets with a completely different tone and style.

La Grande Epicerie de Paris, No Frills (Canada), Wholefoods (Chicago)

Formula and brand oriented communications

Hennes & Mauritz, Bluebird, Sam's wines & spirits, Puma

Not only the store brand, but also the retail branch and the type of store determine tone & style. The atmosphere at a discounter's is different than at a specialist's, and at a brown and white goods store different again than at a jewelry store. Just compare the three supermarkets in the photographs.

2. Focus on Function

Literally, this means all signposting, departmental signs, and service signs. Figuratively, it's the routing, arrangement and layout of the store. It goes without saying that the routing, arrangement and layout of the store must be based on logic – a logic that is often arrived at after a necessary amount of puzzling. With smaller shops the emphasis is more on arrangement and layout; routing plays a greater role with department stores and other large stores.

Sometimes routing is very strict, sometimes it is left up to whim of the customer. For instance, Ikea has a very fixed route, which takes you past every department and which is difficult to avoid (unless

Ikea (Chicago);
a well organized and inspiring
store, partly because of its good
use of instore communications
means.

you know the shortcuts). Strikingly enough, they have made the route much less compulsory in their new venue in Chicago, yet people usually seem to want to walk the whole route. Furthermore, in the Chicago store a lot more impulse products (small products that you can immediately take with you) can be found along the route, and not just at the end anymore – because by that time people have often already forgotten what they had thought was so nice.

Signing makes the arrangement and routing clear to the customer. Sometimes floor plans are desirable, sometimes it is sufficient to name the departments at the spot, depending upon the size of the store. The pictures show a number of examples of highly individualized forms of functional

signing, for even in something as trivial as pointing out the way, you can reveal your personality.

3. Focus on the Product

This information 'replaces' the staff to an important extent, but can be used by them as a memory aid. The idea is for customers to learn as much as possible – without help – about the products and product groups. It is always very important to provide good information in terms of content and to communicate the price, but retailers can do more than that. Inspire the customers. For example, by showing the brand atmosphere of the product within the store brand atmosphere. In supermarkets this sometimes occurs simply by putting products of the same producer together, so that the packaging plays a role. But you can also inspire customers by telling the story of the origin of products or an anecdote about the production process, or you can show what kind of combinations can be made with the product.

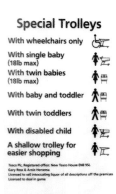

Functionally oriented
communication

Citadium,
Sainsbury,
Next,
Tesco,
CB2

Product oriented communications

Jacob Jensen watch, Dominion (Toronto), Muji (London), Concerto (Amsterdam)

4. Focus on Promotion

In many cases this is the only level of instore communications (apart from pricing perhaps), that is launched in stores. Promotional communications are possible at store level, department level and product level.

At store level, sales campaigns can be tied to a theme; this is a more sympathetic way of presenting special offers than big price cuts alone. Compare this with the promotional possibilities of producer brands: the options there are more or less limited to introductions of new products and promotions of new varieties in taste, or an ordinary special *à la* 3 for the price of 2. A store can more easily take advantage of seasons and holidays or come up with totally individual, perhaps annually recurring themes.

Sales oriented communications

De Bijenkorf during the 'Drie Dwaze Dagen', Container Store

At such moments a store can explore the breadth of its character, do something crazy, something exciting, something unexpected. It can temporarily look totally different, but in such a way that this fits within the personality of the store. A storewide theme can also be employed for ordinary clearance sales and give them added value in that manner. A beautiful example of this are the 'Drie Dwaze Dagen' at the Bijenkorf (Three Daft Days at the Beehive). This department store in the Netherlands operates in a high segment of the market. For three days the Bijenkorf is bright yellow, and all over the store there are crazy, incredible bargains. Yet it remains the Bijenkorf, even though completely different people have now been attracted to the store (bargain hunters).

TO SUMMARIZE

Besides the necessity of communicating with the consumer at these four levels, both the personality of the brand (which represents the emotional values) and the rational information must be recognizable. The relationship between these two ingredients will differ per expression. However, in terms of tone & style all instore communications should be in keeping with the starting points of the formula, with the store's own idiom and 'way of doing things'.

Unfortunately, brand personality is often pretty hard to discern. There might be a lack of balance between the four levels, or one or more levels will be missing. In such cases, this lag in the development of instore communications most likely will stem from:

- Underestimation of the power of instore communications. Whereas research shows that 80% of purchasing decisions are made within the store.
- Lack of knowledge about searching, finding and buying behavior.
- Not meeting the test criteria: addressing (touching a latent desire), advising (in other words, the replacement of the vanished salesperson) and activating and inspiring (prompting).

The longer a shopper remains in a store, the more he or she will buy. And the amount of time a shopper spends in a store depends on how comfortable and enjoyable the experience is. *Paco Underhill*

THE PROCESS OF SEARCHING, FINDING AND BUYING

Searching, finding and buying behavior is heavily dependent on what kind of 'shopping mood' people are in. Are they shopping or just running a quick errand? That is, is it fun shopping or shopping on the run, or an in-between form and thus a little bit of both? The same store will have consumers engaged in shopping in all these ways, although one store will undoubtedly attract more errand runners and another store more fun seekers. What remains true for every store, however, is that the journey through it must be clear and inspiring and that the satisfiers outweigh the dissatisfiers. The fact is, shopping is associated with pleasant aspects – the shopping itself, the inspiration you can get, the products you find in an enjoyable atmosphere, etc. – but also with less pleasant aspects – it takes effort and money and sometimes you are treated badly. The ratio between these positive and negative elements will have to turn out favorably, for then a customer will have had a good experience and be left with positive memories. This ratio is expressed in the customer value formula. More can be read about this formula on the following page.

By now, the different elements of a store formula have been discussed. Together they make the store what it is. Only, the relationship between those components might be in danger of disappearing from view in the meantime. Accordingly the 'Platform Development®' model, which we have already reviewed in chapter 4, will be the subject of the next chapter. The model shows the holistic character of store formulas.

CUSTOMER SATISFACTION AND CREATING CUSTOMER VALUE

from: Waardestrategieën, Service Management magazine, Januari 2000, &Samhoud; and Creatie van klantwaarde, Detailhandelmagazine, February 2001, Henk Gianotten, Professor of Retail Marketing

Buying always goes hand in hand with 'satisfiers' and 'dissatisfiers'. People buy with a specific goal or purpose in mind, but also often for the fun of it. Henk Gianotten makes a distinction between intrinsic customer value and extrinsic customer value, the values that influence a customer's assessment of the 'store experience'. Extrinsic value concerns the product or service, or experience with that product or service. It's about practicality and functionality. Intrinsic value is hedonistic. It's about perception, the pleasure of the shopping experience. The store environment plays an important part in this.

People who are more focused on expediency will experience satisfiers and dissatisfiers in a different way than those who shop purely for pleasure. However, fun shopping and shopping on the run are not opposites. They are rather two separate dimensions in which a person can make a score and hit the jackpot, as it were. A high score for the purpose and functionality of shopping and products can go together with a high score for shopping pleasure and emotionality.

In any event, a consumer must deal with both the aggravating aspects of buying (money and effort) and the pleasant aspects of buying (results, process and emotion). A store formula can create added value in comparison with competitors when it offers the most favourable ratio between satisfiers and dissatisfiers, and when it simultaneously ensures that this ratio works out favourably for both shoppers and targeted customers. Customer satisfaction thus involves the proper balance between expectation & surprise and satisfiers & dissatisfiers. This is expressed in the customer value formula:

$$\frac{Result + Process + Emotion}{Price + Effort} = Customer\ Value$$

Result	Process	Emotion	Price	Effort
• Offer(product, service, core package offers, total offer) • Facilities • Infrastructure	• Supply Processes (distribution channels, systems) • Interaction Moments (reliability, competence) • Tangibles	• Image • Design and Servicescapes • Complaint Settlement • Emotional Binding	• Pricing • Price Fluctuation • Price Differentiation	• Time, energy, attention • Troubles • Uncertainty • Insecurity

What this ultimately entails is that customers get 'value for money' (or believe that they do, in any case). In other words, the advantages (satisfiers) outweigh the disadvantages (dissatisfiers). These factors will hold different importance for different people. What always remains true, however, is that the ultimate 'value' must be positive. The more positive the better, naturally.

In other words, customer value is a consumer's relative perception of each component of the above formula. This perception determines a decision to buy products or services from a retailer. The total experience is the issue.

Gianotten makes a further distinction between Hedonistic Customer Value and the Utilitarian Customer Value. Both bring customers satisfaction, although this is derived from different sources.

A customer derives hedonistic value from:
- sensory perceptions: scent, taste, sound, touch, beauty, aesthetics
- newness: innovation and uniqueness, ambiguity, ambivalence, spontaneity, uncertainty and risk, difference, dynamics
- alternation: diversity and variety, experiences, entertainment, expressiveness, escapism
- nostalgia, authenticity, cultural values, stories
- quality and craftsmanship

A customer derives utilitarian value from:
- convenience: speed, alertness, accessibility
- standardization and uniformity
- certainty and elimination of risk
- functionality

To clarify, in the words of Gianotten:
"Store formulas are in essence nothing more than a promise to consumers that their expectations about the store will prove true, and thus lower their search expenses. However, search expenses are just one element of total customer value. A not unimportant element when consumers undertake goal-oriented activities. But when a consumer sets out to have new experiences and is looking for suspense and excitement, too much uniformity will have a boomerang effect. Higher search expenses can then actually increase customer value."

07

Platform Development®; a model

THE HOLISTIC APPROACH TO RETAIL BRANDING

People are generally inclined to split a store formula into easy to handle components, or disciplines, so that they can then be farmed out to different internal and external parties. This might result in a more orderly, often linear process and clearer descriptions of tasks, but it muddies an overview of the whole process.

HOLISTIC APPROACH

A second disadvantage is the danger that the interpretation of each component will start leading a life of its own, which results in a lack of coherence. We shall have to deal with this paradox: unravelling the 'formula complexity', but the same time continuing to see the formula as a whole.

This chapter will be devoted entirely to a model. This model, Platform Development®, refers to the actual realization of the store formula.

It is used in order to give insight into the importance of a clear and complete brand concept and to show that the development of a store formula is a holistic affair. All components of a formula stand in relation to one another.

Most formulas in retailing are simple, it's keeping them up day to day that is difficult.

Gordon Seagull (founder of Crate & Barrel)

It is clear by now that identity is comprised of an emotional and a rational aspect. The rational corporate values can be copied by competitors, but the combination of corporate values and personality produces the emotional aspect, which is inherent and unique to a company. This idea is important to keep in mind when interpreting the Platform Development® model.

THE ELEMENTS, THE CORE AND THE BOUNDARY

In developing the brand concept, all components of the formula are important. All of the formula elements in this model come together around the core, that is, the brand. The elements can accordingly be manipulated from this midpoint and made to work together. The 'brand' therefore contains the earlier mentioned rational and emotional values. The ambitions form the circumference of the circle. That is what we are working toward.

Figure 1a (on the next page) contains the elements that will have to be examined (at a certain point). Which of these are most important can differ per retail formula. Logically, it would seem handy to tackle those aspects first. But in fact, the elements can be dealt with randomly, in different tempos and oftens imultaneously, as long as they all are dealt with. There is no real hierarchy. The only hierarchy that there is, is that the brand steers the formula. That's why everyone who has an influence on the elements of the formula (initiator, manager, etc.) must be associated with the core. Which at any event comes down to the brand owner, the management, the brand manager or a (possibly partially external) brand team.'

In retail, the brand actually represents the truth in all aspects of the formula.

formula concept / ambition

SERVICE
Pre-purchase:
- Communications plan
Supplementary services:
- e.g. day care
Post-purchase:
- Repairs
- Customizing (tailoring)
- Credit (satisfaction or
  your money back)

ASSORTMENT
- Basic/collection/peripheral
- Store brand in relation to
  product brand
- Exclusive brands
- Product range
  (breadth, depth)
- New producs,
  latest/newest trends
- Packaging
- Tempo of replenishment
- Quality (material,
  professionality, design)
- Distribution structure,
  supply management,
  transport

**MASS-MEDIA
COMMUNICATIONS**
- Selection of media
  channels
- Promotional goals
- Sponsoring, campaigns,
  promotional activities
- Themes
- Timing
- Promotional budget

EXPERIENCE
- Expectations vs. surprise
- Fixed and dynamic
  elements
- Creating conversion value
- Attraction
- Fulfilment
- Customer journey

STAFF
- Training, selection,
  professional knowledge
- Behaviour
- Clothing
- Tone of address

**INSTORE
COMMUNICATIONS**
- Tone & style
- Brand identity
- Logo
- Focus on formula and brand
- Focus on product: products
  and product groups
- Signposting
- Themes, campaigns

VISUAL MERCHANDISING
- Point-of-sale material,
  displays
- Presentation of goods
- Store window

STORE
- Design
- Functional starting points/
  layout
- Routing
- Façade/store front
- Lighting, sound, fragrance

PRICE
- Maximum-minimum
- Price structure
- Campaigns
- Absolute price level
  (margin-mix)
- Pricing methods (volume
  discounts, on credit, etc.)
- Price image
- Relative price level
  (price recognition)

LOCATION
- Choice for: city centre, outer
  districts, city outskirts,
  shopping centre, etc.
- Multiformat/multichannel
- Coverage
- Transport
- International

Figuur 1a. All components of the Platform Development® model

THE FORMULA CONCEPT

As mentioned earlier, the ambitions form the circumference of the outer circle, the boundary. This is the specified goal that you work toward, or in other words the stated concept of the formula.

The formula concept establishes what must be realized per element for a specific store formula.

The idea is to fill in all parts, for a filled-in part means that that element of the formula has been lived up to.

The formula elements are already completely or partially filled in at the start of the project, a representation of the current situation. An inventory of each formula element will clarify whether that element should be completely changed, modified, or can stay the way it is.

It should be noted here that the outside circle is not a kind of 'maximum score', which can only be reached in the most ideal circumstances, but is precisely what we wish to achieve.

For example, when personnel do not play an important role (rare, but possible) or, as suggested, has already been worked out sufficiently, then that part can immediately be filled in completely. For the boundary of the formula concept will have already been reached.

MAKING AN INVENTORY
OF THE ELEMENTS

At the beginning of an assignment it is often not completely clear to what extent an element of the formula has already been worked out. The more that is known about the direction in which the brand concept is heading, the more possible it is to make a more accurate inventory. An example is given in Figure 1b. A desire for renewal will in many cases arise when a brand begins to lose its ties with the changing society. The difficulty, however, is that with a new store design alone, for example, it is not possible to successfully catch up. Adapting one element means that it is extremely likely that other elements will also have to change along with it.

Now, it is difficult to get to grips with all elements at the same time, because of the separation of disciplines mentioned earlier. You can give advice to a retailer from the point of view of the brand in order to guarantee the consistency of the image as much as possible. In practice, however, it often

proves to be up to the entrepreneur whether to follow that advice or not. The pragmatic attitude entrepreneurs often have can sometimes push the brand idea to the background. Decisions are then based on considerations of cost or the need for quick turnover.

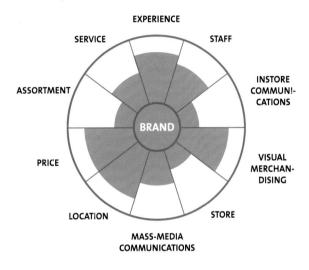

Figuur 1b. Example of an inventory of the formula elements

UNBALANCED ASSORTMENT

Making an inventory of the elements can bring various symptoms to light, as the example of Figure 1c shows. One element (in this case the assortment) can be developed too far or unevenly. There can be products in the assortment that run ahead of developments in the market or that do not fit inwith the formula, or products can be lacking which have become essential for the formula.

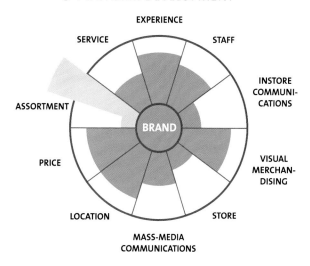

Figuur 1c. An unevenly developed assortment

ARBITRARY DEVELOPMENT OF ELEMENTS

Another example has been pictured in Figure 1d. One component of the mass-media communications develops beyond the bounds of the formula – a magazine, for instance. The parameters for this magazine are not determined by the needs of the brand, the target group or commercial objectives, but by the thought, "What sort of magazine do we like...."

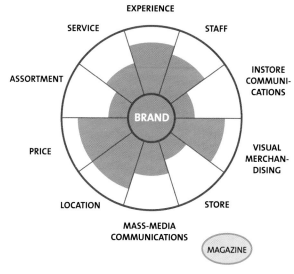

Figuur 1d. Example of a magazine developed outside the scope of the formula

THE PILOT STORE

A following important benchmark is the realization of the pilot store. This store is one of the elements, but in addition to that it is the physical container of the entire formula. All elements of the formula come together within it. In the ideal situation, all elements are completely worked out and realized in the pilot store, so that the effect of the whole can be studied. More often, however, some elements will remain underdeveloped. Because of a lack of time, for instance (adapting the assortment happens to take a lot of time) or because the effect of failing to do so is underestimated.

It sometimes happens that after the realization of the pilot store, development stops. It is important to realize that the pilot store is not an endpoint but simply a starting point. Here again, making an inventory of the elements provides much insight.

What shape are we in with the new store, have we realized our ambitions? People sometimes have the tendency to explain disappointing results by saying that the store is no good, whereas the problem probably lies in the fact that the elements are out of balance. Because of this, it is important to see the pilot store as a test case. The exact cause of the problem can then be discovered and solved.

The process is the product. It's a never-ending story!

THE PROCESS IS THE PRODUCT

After an evaluation, it can turn out that it is necessary to take a step back in rolling out the concept. Elements can perish because of operational or practical problems. The consequence of this is that the actual boundary of the formula will have to be pulled back somewhat. At that point the original boundary of the formula can sooner be called an ideal picture.

Figure 1e demonstrates this. The starting points could be less further developed and perhaps even partially changed. The new outer circle then becomes an adapted version of the old outer circle. And although the starting points of each may be different, this will not be a difference of day and night.

These developments cannot be prevented, and they are also not serious. But it is important that you are aware of them and deal with them judiciously. All elements will have to be pulled back (on a more positive note, adjusted) so that they all end up on

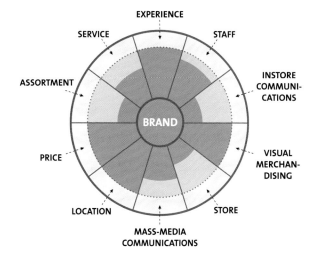

Figuur 1e. A pulled-back formula boundary

the same, new level – for the circle must remain round. Only then does the formula work again.

Figure 1f shows that a store formula will never (or should never) cease developing. After all, we live in a changing society, which is changing faster and faster, for that matter. During the life cycle of a store formula, large steps (but especially many small ones) will be taken to introduce change. A new store situation can of course be considered a large step – a revolution. As a result the entire formula is tackled, as has been illustrated in the previous examples. In most cases this has consequences for all of the elements.

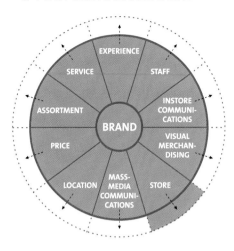

Figuur 1f. Continued development of the formula: a revolution

Figuur 1g. Continued development of the formula: an evolution

In the case of a small step, an evolution, the changes will mainly occur in one, or perhaps only a few, areas; for example, an adaptation of the logo. The rest of the formula will still be sufficient and it will not always be necessary to tackle the other elements at that time. The advantage of all these small evolutions is their contribution to a fresh, innovative retail formula with a position in the midst of the market. In the model, the elements which have no need of renewal can be extended to the new boundary. For they meet the demands of the new formula concept. See Figure 1g.

INSIGHT

We would like to emphasize an important insight once again here: Changing one element will result (very likely) in all elements having to be changed. With one of our clients, the stopping power of the formula (the pilot store) had increased considerably. But the conversion lagged behind expectations. The personnel did not know how to deal with the enormous amount of visitors in the store. Extra training was sorely needed. And even though the problem had been pinpointed and discussed at an earlier stage, only when the store actually opened did the effect of such a change become visible and convincing.

Retailing 101 starts with the notion that a store has three distinct aspects: design (meaning the premises), merchandising (whatever you put in them) and operations (whatever employees do). These Big Three, while seemingly separate, are in fact completely intertwined, interrelated and interdependent, meaning that when somebody makes a decision regarding one, a decision has been made about the other two as well. *Paco Underhill*

IN CONCLUSION

Reality is always difficult to capture in models. But models do give a lot of insight into the material at hand and the problems that can arise.

What takes centre stage in the retail formula is the holistic approach. All elements of the formula come together in the physical store. To realize successful renewal it is important to chart the relationship of those elements, starting from the defined brand concept. In effecting this renewal, it is important to recognize that the pilot store is a challenge: it is a starting point instead of a finishing point.

The practical examples show that an unbalanced development of elements or the development of elements outside the scope of the brand can produce an inconsistent image, which can have adverse effects on the consumer's experience of the formula. And that a formula should never stop developing, whether that be in large or small steps.

Besides the complexity that the holistic character of a store formula entails, when considered realistically every project will have to deal with its setbacks. Models cannot prevent setbacks, but what they can do is contribute to altering them in a positive sense. A setback is also not a finishing point. What it does is provide just that more drive to improve solutions (or, in this case, elements of the formula) and to estimate the possible consequences even better the next time.

08

The Changing Society

RETAIL REFLECTS SOCIETY: ACT AND REACT, OR SUFFER

Ten years ago, who would have thought that half the people in Holland would now be walking around with a tattoo or piercing? What once only had been reserved for or aspired to by swaggering sailors and greasy machos has now become widely accepted. And as is always the case with trends and social developments, sooner or later it will be 'out' again, too. With all the ensuing problems, but also new developments – the methods to get rid of those tattoos.

Developing a retail formula has more to do with everyday life and our changing society than with stores in themselves.

Getting henna tattoos in the middle of Selfridges. What's next?

But for now, tattoo and piercing shops are still popping up everywhere like mushrooms. The shops that were once located in disreputable back streets can now be found in the centres of cities. In Las Vegas I saw a girl getting a tattoo on her back; her face was drawn with pain as she sat there in the display window. In the photo only henna tattoos are being made, to be sure, but this is in the middle of Selfridges in London. Because those who don't want to, or dare to, take the step for a real tattoo (and above all are often not *allowed* to on their parents' orders) can get by with stick-on, brush-on, or henna tattoos that last a few weeks, or fake piercings that you can clamp on.

'When I started tattooing, there were six of us in Holland (mid '70s). Now there are hundreds on every street corner…. I had a little shop in the red light district and it was a sailor's paradise, full of adventure… but now the person who wants a tattoo – along with everyone else in the world – has turned into a sort of Lenny Kravitz type with weird coloured sunglasses and low slung pants who want a little spaghetti curl tattooed just above and below the crack in their ass. The rowdy sailors who stank of booze and the bleached blond whores, the classic tattoo cellars with the ship in the bottle and other mementoes of a seafaring life – that doesn't exist anymore.'

Henk Schiffmacher ('tattoo king')

Ikea: 'This is a Grand Foulard.
Drape it over a couch. Nice idea, eh?!'

IKEA CHANGES EVERYTHING

Changes that have a real influence on society come from different, often unpredictable quarters. And an important motivating force, something which can be perceived earlier or more easily, is a feeling of restlessness or discontent in the market, for change entails a breeding ground for change.

The arrival of Ikea sparked a great change in how we live in and furnish our homes. Ikea established its branch in the Netherlands about 25 years ago. Before that, there was only the furniture strip and speciality home furnishing shops. Young people decorated their homes with leftover furniture from their parents in the same fashion as their parents: traditional. Ikea became known as a cheap supplier of do-it-yourself kits; later on 'ready-made' products were introduced which were likewise affordable. The assortment consisted (and still consists) of a broad palette of styles, ranging from modern to timeless to classical. This made it possible for young people to have interiors with an individual flavour without having to dig deep in their pockets. On top of that, Ikea had truly new ideas, such as the grand foulards shown in the photo. If we designers had gone to a manufacturer/shopkeeper with the idea of a 'grand foulard' (before Ikea had made this product popular), they would have said: "Our clients never ask for that!" Whereas Ikea says: "This is a grand foulard, you can use it like this. Nice idea, eh? And: "Take it or leave it, its up to you."

The consequences for the furniture market were enormous. A number of companies stubbornly went on in the traditional manner and didn't make it in the by-now changed society. But other companies took inspiration from Ikea and evolved, and became the better for it. A relatively overlooked market had been cultivated and would start to grow.

What Ikea drew with it in its wake was a new-found acceptance and even hunger for design, which led to the rise of many new initiatives such as home decorating shops, bathroom shops, thingummy shops, etc. The consequences of this have extended into various other media – witness the countless home decorator magazines and television programs. The photo shows Jan des Bouvrie, the icon of Dutch interior design, teaching the young girl in the picture to become an aspiring interior architect. In this way a demand is created amongst the girl and her peers, which traditional furniture stores will no longer be able to fulfil 10 years down the road. The need for the development of new or evolving concepts is constant.

One of the countless lifestyle
programs on television

The effect that these changes in society have on the store picture is enormous: a great variety in the type of stores as well as variety in the content of the different formulas.

PROCESSES OF CHANGE

The changes that Ikea brought about in the furniture market occurred extremely rapidly. However, this was not a total concept that was put into effect overnight, but developed gradually and, in retrospect, very logically. Ikea was there with the right products in the right context at the right moment. It played on the dissatisfaction in the market with the furniture branch. A dissatisfaction that became more widespread once people got wise to the fact that things could be done otherwise. Ikea was, and is, successful because they see where customers are at and because they do things their own way. But not everything can be predicted: some initiatives did not catch on (a few product lines, for example) and others have been more successful than expected. It also turns out that a relatively boring basic article like the familiar 'Billy' system of closets and shelving can remain in the assortment for many years. Which in itself is a good thing, for such product continuity makes the development of new products financially possible.

In general, the public's acceptance of such developments is relatively capricious and is group related. The curve of 'The Adoption Process' shows that people vary in their readiness to adopt an innovation. The Harvard Design School Guide to Shopping succinctly summarizes this process: "The look created by urban 'innovators,' considered the adventurous ones, can be said to spread to a small group of style attentive 'early adopters,' then to a larger constituency, the 'early majority,' and then pass on to the sceptical but ultimately accepting suburban masses, or 'late majority,' and finally to anyplace and no place, to the 'laggards.'"

Social changes need time to develop and a constant interaction between market and supplier. Whereas product and market trends are of shorter duration and often unpredictable – they can sometimes suddenly catch on like wildfire.

CHANGES IN COOKING AND EATING HABITS

Another striking example of our changing society is our cooking and eating habits, which have changed in terms of tastes, ingredients and preparation. The many contacts with foreign cuisine in this country, our love of travel, but also the initiatives of supermarkets have helped make this possible. Our behaviour has also changed in terms of when and where we eat as a result of far-reaching changes in our social habits. This is partly due to the influence of television with all of its cooking programs, the recipe columns in newspapers and magazines (that have become increasingly exotic) and the free cooking magazines that are given out at supermarkets.

Changes in family makeup – double-income families (with or without children), single person households, the relatively well off over-fifties – have an influence on our living patterns. They lead to other needs and consequentially to other behaviour. As far as cooking goes, it is a well-known fact that the time that people spend on it has shortened drastically. According to research done at the British Imperial College, this will have been reduced to eight minutes by 2010. And although it is truethat knowledge and expertise in cooking and its métier is disappearing, the demand for more delicious meals with greater variety is rising! Having a quick bite during the week (with instant or almost instant meals having to be high quality, wholesome and tasty) and cooking elaborately for friends in the weekend: that's the new lifestyle. Whereas friends used to visit each other for coffee or drinks in the evening, now they exchange the most incredible recipes at the dinner table.

The effect that these changes have had on the store picture is enormous: a great variety in the type of stores as well as variety in the content of the different formulas.

Besides the food itself, the moments at which people eat have also become flexible. The traditional three meals a day is being replaced by 'grazing', in other words eating little bites throughout the day wherever you happen to be at the time. Refreshment stands along the way, school canteens, convenience stores, petrol stations – the choices are legion. This has also had its effect on supermarkets. Turnover has dropped steadily, because people can only eat but so much a day and spend their money but once. New strategies are inevitably the result – proof of the enormous influence society and retail have upon each other.

We are at a time in history when brands go beyond being business platforms to becoming symbols of our times. Brands like McDonalds, Sony and Budweiser often reflect the changing values of our society. Brands are more than just advertising, they are part of our culture.

© 2002 Harvest Communications LLC

THE RETAIL BRAND IN OUR CHANGING SOCIETY

Store formulas must continually ask themselves what relevance they have for the consumer at that specific juncture in time. And also what relation there is between what they offer, how their brand is experienced, and what role this plays in people's daily lives. Being in step with society does not automatically mean that everything has to be 'modern'. A brand experience can easily be traditional or authentic without losing relevance. However there must always be a contemporary and progressive aspect present within the formula and character of the brand. Witness the revival of Burberry.

A retail brand cannot be considered separately from all aspects of the retail formula. The previous chapter provided elucidation on the holistic character of the retail formula. All formula elements together with the underlying principals form an inseparable whole. What we want to add in this chapter is that the whole must function within society. And so we say, 'Retail reflects society. Act and react, or suffer!'

How is it possible to build a brand in an environment where everything, including competitors, distributors and consumers, is in a constant state of change? It's the brand's paradox: Survival means change.

Jean-Noël Kapferer

There are plenty of examples of chains that have lost their relevance in society in one way or another. Consider the struggle that C&A is going through, with the low point being the closed stores in England. The photo shows the store premises in Oxford Street, 4000 or 5000 m2 empty, with the shadow of the C&A logo still just barely visible. Shocking!

And the other way around, all those formulas from abroad such as Marks & Spencer, Argos, Habitat and Boots that could not make any headway in the Netherlands. Each of them very strong brands in their own region, but they were unable to link up with cultures on the continent. A lack in terms of empathy and adjustment, for when in Rome, do as the Romans do.

But it can also be otherwise. Formulas such as Hennes & Maurits, The Bodyshop, Mango and Zara do manage to make such a link and they are very successful in doing so. Although in all fairness, these are formulas with a global character that take

Oxford Street, London: the shadow of the C&A logo, still barely visible, after C&A withdrew in 2001

A Burberry Addict

advantage of what is relevant at this juncture in time. They have not stemmed from local traditions and do not have traditional brand values. That gives them the possibility of keeping up with the times. Although time will tell.

What time will also tell is how fast this chapter will become outdated. The changing society never stands still, whereas this chapter must wait another half year before it is printed and lying on the bookstore shelves. A lot can happen in even such a short time. But although the examples we'd then cite would probably be different, the ideas remain the same along general lines.

Treat fashion as if it were perishable produce: keep it fresh, and keep it moving. That means spotting the trends even before the trendoids do, turning the ideas into fashionable clothes, and making the apparel fly off the racks.

Stefan Persson (chairman of H&M)

Retail reflects society.
Act and React,
or Suffer.

09

Retail renewal & Retail innovation

THE WAY TO A NEW CONCEPT

Renewal and innovation are vitally important for a brand in our rapidly changing society. This does not mean that you have to run after those changes, so to speak, in the retail formula. What the formula must do is map out its own future, follow its own path, guided by its own personality.

THE DNA OF A BRAND

The uniqueness of a store brand stems for a large part from its identity. That is the fountainhead from which a retail organization can operate and profile itself. This fits in with the views of Dr. Klaus Brandmeyer, who has written an extensive treatise on the genetic code of brands. The DNA of a brand is the basis of a company's success. Managements come and go, but the brand will always be there. A management has only temporary control over the course a company must steer and the way in which the brand must be presented in the market. All too often a new management will want to put its stamp on the company, making decisions on the basis of 'doing things differently' instead of on the basis of the brand identity. The result is that 'unnatural' steps are taken at the cost of the DNA. A management is the temporary administrator of a brand, not the owner.

With some companies, and often with family businesses, the founder of the company is also the brand owner. Think, for instance, of founders Ingvar Kamprad of Ikea and Sam Walton of Wal-Mart. Ingvar *is* Ikea and Sam *is* Wal-Mart (even though by now this is '*was*'). Now, this could easily result in a very limited and rigid identity, but what these two men have in common is that they are very aware of developments in the market and take advantage of this from the standpoint of the corporate identity. They also stayed involved with the enterprise for as long as possible, if no longer as part of management then for instance as member of the Board of Directors. In this way they could correct, guide and take over for the new management if the brand identity were in danger of being bypassed. They made sure that the original emotional values that they had given to the company are well established and still being observed. Wal-Mart has 'Sam Walton's rules', and the following anecdote (from www.brandhome.nl) says a lot about Ingvar Kamprad.

"Through all sorts of complicated constructions, Kamprad has insured that his concept is strictly protected after his death and that his three sons can in no way whatsoever mess up their father's work. In 1986, at the age of 66, he resigned as general manager. Nevertheless, he remained active here and there. Kept on checking all across the world whether his holy principles were being properly observed. The 'devilishly vigilant' Kamprad would unexpectedly show up in an Ikea store at 5:30 in the morning, and then first speak with the people who had come to deliver the goods. How were the safety precautions? What irritated them the most? Had they been offered coffee? In his spot checks and inspections, which sometimes lasted 13 hours, it turned out that people always expressed the same 100 to 200 complaints. These he categorized and then worked on."

Although brand identity is the guiding factor, that in itself is not enough reason to preserve the brand. Preservation simply results in the brand being put on the shelf to gather dust, until at a certain point the use-by date is passed. Renewal and innovation are vitally important for a brand in these fast-changing times, but success will only follow when the identity is at the foundation of the new steps to be taken.

Markets are generally defined as too 'limited' with the result that the competition is judged in terms of that narrow market, whereas clients are generally considered rationally acting individuals.

Henk Gianotten (Professor of Retail Marketing)

DEFINING THE FOUNDATION FOR CHANGE

The fact that identity is also a guiding factor in the (retail) brand choices that people make is the subject of chapter 3. Although in reality it is the image of the brand which guides consumers, for after all that is how consumers perceive you. Accordingly, image should be a logical consequence of identity. If it is the other way around (with image determining identity), then you become the plaything of consumers and are at the mercy of their whims. One of the essentials we can glean from that chapter is that a corporation can make itself eligible through its identity. Therefore renewal must also be based on the personality, for consumers will have chosen your brand for certain reasons. When they no longer understand its behaviour because other values suddenly apply, they will choose another brand that does come across clearly.

In that chapter we also talked about Kapferer's identity prism, a method of discovering the corporate identity and putting it into words. This prism is also useful as part of the renewal process because of the clear overview it gives of the breakdown of the process (physique, personality, culture, relation, reflected customer, customer self-concept). It gives insight into which elements must remain unchanged because they are an essential foundation of the identity and which elements can be elevated to a higher level that aspires to more. In order to institute a change, however, an in-depth investigation of identity is not enough itself. Positioning and external market factors play a large role as to the direction that renewal takes.

Market positioning can be determined through normal marketing devices, such as a strengths/weaknesses analysis with regard to the organization, and an opportunities/threats analysis with regard to society. The changed society with all of its developments (sociological, demographical, political, cultural etc.) plays a large role here. The Unique Buying Reasons and the Unique Selling Propositions will also come into play. Here, however, what will above all be revealed are similarities with other suppliers, for uniqueness can only come into being when the Buying Reasons and Selling Propositions are connected with the brand personality.

Porter's Five Forces Model also provides insight. This model looks at the competition within a brand's own segment, what new suppliers/entrants can be expected, the power of suppliers, the power of buyers, and possible substitutes. The model maps out what forces exist and which can be developed further. It makes clear how attractive the position of the enterprise actually is and what elements have an influence on it.

Everything comes together in the mission statement. It is the most concise description of the brand. It contains the identity, with its emotional values; the positioning, which has a rational basis; and the ambition and vision, which are the guiding line for the coming years. The mission statement provides answers to questions such as: Who are our clients? What is our business now, and what will it be in the future?

The true winners are the companies that approach consumers through different channels and search for where they can add value.

Marc de Swaan Arons
(founder of EffectiveBrands,
a marketing consultancy)

You have to define the foundation to begin with. You clean up the rubble, get the foundation right and then you can build.

Vittorio Radice (CEO Selfridges)

All of those words will ultimately have to be translated into concrete form in the renewed retail formula, which is a principally visual environment. And so the words will have to be transposed into colours, forms and graphic images. This can sometimes cause problems when both parties do not have the same image of the word 'chic' or 'value for money', for instance. With the help of image exercises it is possible to create a common framework of reference. This too is an essential part of establishing the current identity and the desired new direction.

THE CONSUMER AND THE BRAND

In the fervour of defining the identity and the direction of the new concept, it is important to keep the consumers in sight at all times. For soon they will have to feel drawn to the entire proposition, the triad upon which the brand is built: identity, market position and ambition. The symbiosis between consumer and company is partially responsible for the success of the formula.

Consumers base their shopping choices on the combination of what is offered, who offers it and how it is offered. That's where the wellspring of the concept lies. The wellspring of the concept seldom lies in the product itself because unique products are rare, and successful products seldom remain rare. By offering products in a specific context they become unique. That context can be defined by asking yourself what your products can mean for consumers, both rationally and emotionally. Such meaning can arise at the moment of purchase or use by making a link with a lifestyle, for example, or by offering surprising combinations. This, together with who you are, your unique identity, is what makes the difference.

With a clear-cut proposition, a retailer will appeal to specific groups of people, people whose attitudes toward life probably are rather similar. On the other hand, certain groups will not buy because they do not feel addressed. Not because the company adopts an attitude of being choosy, but precisely because it makes itself eligible.

Victoria's Secret
A big step:
from extremely prim to
distinctive and sensual

Now, most retail companies seem to know very well what types of people buy from them. As a matter of fact, that often proves to be a reflection of the people in the company itself. This confirms the view that a brand is a platform for kindred spirits. A compatibility that is felt between people outside the company, but also between people who work in the company and between both of these groups. People experience the appreciation that comes from their specific group as if it were a tonic; they need it in order to keep going in this complex world of ours.

In order to continue serving that core target group well, a retail concern must know how their clients behave, what things they like, how they live, etc. This is a group that you don't want to lose because of a renewed concept. Moreover, it is also important to find out which adjacent groups might be interested in the new proposition and what meaning the products can have for those new groups. New relations can arise in this way, based on the communication of a certain communal feeling, so that consumers recognize kindred spirits. It is therefore important to actively search out what communality is considered desirable or innovative and what lies within the scope of the brand. For when the company itself is not enthusiastic about certain ideas or products and the work that this entails, this will be evident and consumers will not be convinced. The motto of our company is based on this fundamental principle: "Inspire yourself, inspire your customer."

The real value of a brand lies in its ability to persuade and please consumers. This does not necessarily mean that the best product or service will always win over consumers, but rather that the knowledge of what consumers need, how they behave, what they think, how they perceive value and how they reason and decide defines such outcomes.

Sicco van Gelder
(founder of Brand Meta, a brand strategy consultancy)

Dunhill (London)
A recognizably high class
old English style that goes
with Dunhill and yet is very
inspiring for the present age

THE SHOPPER, THE CUSTOMER AND THE CONSUMER

Despite extensive target-group research and despite categorizing all of their desires and their lifestyles, much about customer behaviour remains unpredictable. By no means all shoppers (meaning 'shop visitors') become customers (meaning 'buyers') and the person who uses the product is not always the one who buys it. So whom do you focus on? Moreover, the actual customer, thus the one who buys, is often terribly ambiguous. A few examples:

· Sometimes people opt for healthy food, at another times they go for a fatty treat.
· Sometimes shopping must be done as quickly and efficiently as possible, at other moments customers take their time and read every bit of information.
· Sometimes people want easy-to-prepare or instant meals, at other times they want a culinary tour de force that they prepare all by themselves.
· Sometimes price doesn't matter; sometimes people go to a store for a special offer.

Rodney Fitch, who founded 'Fitch', one of the first retail design agencies and now one of the largest, has formulated five universal core values in relation to customers. These points of interest can be kept in mind when developing a retail formula:

· Customers are all individuals and you should treat them as such. (Which is in keeping with our approach to instore communications requiring a one-to-one approach with the appropriate tone and style.)

- They're all afraid. Afraid of dropping out of their peer group, afraid of the products they buy, afraid of everything under the sun.
- They're all sceptical. (Which is not so surprising, when you keep up with the daily news.) A scepticism and distrust that you will have to recognize and that can only be overcome by displaying continual understanding and honesty.
- They're all very easily distracted. One day you can catch their full attention as a retailer, the next you are boring and they go somewhere else. (Comparable with the ambiguous customer described earlier.) The only thing that the store formula can do is constantly attempt to add something to the life of its customers, so that the formula has a contemporary relevancy.
- They're all design, style and brand driven. (Something we need not emphasize further here.)

CONCEPTING

The foregoing is necessary before real 'concepting' can begin. The concept is loaded from the analysis and description of the brand (identity, positioning and ambition/market division) and the image that this forms of who you are and who you want to be. There are three routes that fill in the concept:

1. The Brand Route
2. The Consumer Route
3. The Communications Route

The Brand Route

The distinguishing elements of the brand are translated into what we call core value, initial value and added value. The core value represents the basic elements of the brand, such as its aura of self-confidence or the knowledge that the company has about the product/service. The initial value reflects the elements that are preconditions, or in other words, those through which the core value is realized or made possible, such as quality and a contemporary air. The added value usually comes from the entire store experience, which is formed by all of the elements together. This produces an image of the store formula in highlights, but includes all of its facets. From the outside to the inside, from large to small, from façade to shelf.

The Consumer Route

In developing the concept, it is important to find the proper angle or angles of approach in order to inspire and enthuse the core customers and adjoining customer groups so that they will come more often and spend more. This of course is directly proportional to how well the core value and the initial value do, but especially to communicating added value. Therefore it is important to discover what it is that moves your target group and desired target group and what will prompt them to buy. Visually, the current target group and the (aspirant) adjoining target groups are pictured in relation to what you offer and are intending to offer. The buying and consuming moments mentioned earlier play a role here, but so do any themes which can influence the behaviour of a consumer (for instance, seasons, holidays or special events in a consumer's life) and the difference between holiday shopping days and a normal winter working day.

The Communications Route

Communications are also manifested through the brand identity. Communication is an important part of the formula, for in order to make the proposition and the added value known, the brand must speak – literally and figuratively, instrumentally and aspirationally. Communication is a part of the process by which a store brand can enter into a relationship with the consumer.

Some people are by nature very good at concepting, but there are also methods which can help us to think more broadly and in different ways. Lateral thinking is very useful in concept development. When, for example, a new concept is being developed for a supermarket, you can look at other branches. How does a department store do things and how does a small super-specialist do it? Then you translate that information into your own concepts. Reinterpretation of developments in the market can provide surprising perspectives, but so can developments in other countries; whether this is explicitly in retail or a global social development, they are all important sources of inspiration.

BRAND IN YOUR HAND®

Another handy aid for concepting is the Brand In Your Hand® model. It is a guideline, developed in order to more specifically seek out the scope and possibilities of the brand. You can do 'out-of-the-box' thinking and ask questions like: Are there any events that can be organized from the brand point of view? Are there any possibilities for new 'special products' that can, for instance, physically represent the emotional values of the brand? What media of your own can you create that can be effective for

communicating the brand values? What possibilities do you have in the area of retail; are different formats necessary in order to optimally serve the customers? This last question is crucial, in view of the fact that differentiation (multiformat/multichannel) is one of the real innovations currently going on in retail land. Many businesses believe they have gone multichannel because they have a website. But that is true 'multichannel' only when the website is a functional service or sales channel. Multiformat goes a step further, which the following chapter will illustrate.

⊕ BRAND IN YOUR HAND®

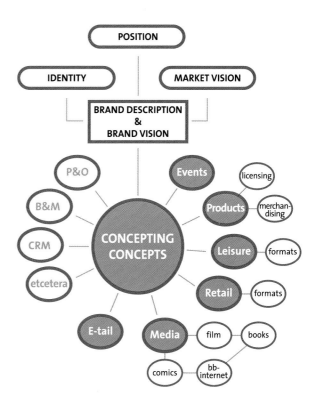

Anthropologie is the new but grown-up little brother of Urban Outfitters.

Urban Outfitters (Toronto)

Anthropologie (New York City)

RETHINKING THE STORE

Although the title of this chapter might suggest otherwise, most developments in retail are more evolutionary (renewal) than revolutionary (innovation). A number of real innovations with tremendous consequences have already been discussed: the introduction of self-service (the many possibilities of which have nowhere near been developed), selling via the Internet (which in fact is still in its infancy), and now the necessity of multiformat/multichannel strategies. This last development is connected with the consumers' desire for more and more convenience, more perception and more pleasure and their increased demands with regard to 'customized service' in which the capacity of the retailer must exactly meet their requirements at that specific moment at that specific place.

As we've said, the majority of these are renewals that are necessary in order to keep up with our changed and changing society. With renewal of the retail concept, the 'rethinking the store' route plays a large part. With renewal a retailer often walks the old beaten tracks: freshened-up presentations of new products, beautifully (re)decorated sales islands, but the 'order picking' still always starts from the high shelves in the aisles. Seldom do retailers break out of this way of thinking and make an inventory of how the order picking process can be better linked to the changed needs of consumers. A retailer traditionally steers the shop from the purchasing point of view, and then the store is the endpoint of the logistical process. Consumers look at this exactly the other way around. They are not concerned with an efficient logistical process (except when they encounter an empty shelf). In principle, however, they have no knowledge of it, nor do they consider it their problem. They want the products to simply be there – in a shop which appeals to the imagination, which meets their expectations, and which can surprise them every now and again. This means that the point of sale has become the company's raison d'être. People in the Western world are able to acquire such an enormous profusion of things in so many places, through direct and indirect channels, that the brand and the sales locales that go with it ultimately offer the only distinction and advantage. That's why it is necessary to inseparably couple purchasing and sales and to steer them from one and the same brand concept.

With 'rethinking the store', ingrained habits and standard ways of thinking and working are reconsidered. The function of the retail formula is defined anew, from the viewpoint of the customer. The central focus is the meaning that the formula must have for the consumer. This can have drastic consequences for an entire branch, which is accustomed to always behaving and presenting itself in a certain manner.

Many people were very sceptical about the strategy of Hennes and Mauritz. No one believed that 'fashion' could be combined with low prices, not even so much from a tactical point of view, but more from the idea that the consumer would not except this.

The true winners are the companies that approach consumers through different channels and search for where they can add value. *Marc de Swaan Arons (founder of EffectiveBrands, a maketing consultancy)*

Oki-ni (London)
A physical Internet store:
touch, try and order.

Siebel Juweliers (old and new),
a large chain in the Netherlands

present or simply to indulge yourself. A drastic turn-around like this will have consequences for the entire jewellery branch, for the other players have suddenly become dated.

'Rethinking the store' is also at the foundation of devising the most fitting strategy for multiformat/multichannel developments. However, not every company is in a position to go that far, or to even apply the concept of 'rethinking the store' in its totality. But a retail company will always have to display a greater than average alertness in order to hold its own in today's society.

Rather different than your average shady sexshop

Another example comes from the jewellers' branch. From time immemorial jewellery stores have been impregnable establishments, a closed black hole in a shopping street. People don't simply go in to browse around and come up with a few ideas, and so very little spontaneous buying behaviour can be expected of the customer. Thus we completely opened things up for a large Dutch jewellery chain, lots of light, lots of glass, no overcrowded windows, but only a few teasers which drew customers inside. The effect was incredible. People who had never even known that a jewellery shop had been at that spot in the street before, have now gained an inspiring place to shop. A shop you can visit not only for really special occasions (marriage, anniversaries, etc.) but also for a birthday

Consumers base their shopping choices on the combination of what is offered, who offers it, and how it is offered. That's where the wellspring of the concept lies.

MOMENT-MOOD MODEL

Specific and universal values

Traditionally, consumers are described by using concrete and distinguishing parameters. This makes the marketing of the product, the service or the store much clearer. Such descriptions are based on culture (in the sense of background or 'roots', but also in the sense of the sub culture(s) in which a person moves), and additionally in terms of age, social class, demography, sex, etc., which is often further supplemented by all sorts of specific information relating to that particular group. Determination of core target groups usually comes from the 'gut feelings' of the trendsetters and decision-makers of the organization and in many cases is supported by research (external or internal) and recommendations from external advisors.

At any rate, it is very useful to draw up a description of your core target group with specific values such as these. Gut feelings and entrepreneurship are generally good mainsprings for a successful enterprise, as long as inspiration comes from contemporary society. Consumers themselves will not find it easy to describe their actions or desires and needs, so that they will never be the direct source of new ideas. But they most certainly are an indirect source, because much information can be gained by observing and analysing them closely. A subsequent interpretation and translation of consumer behaviour in today's society can lead to successful steps and concepts in terms of appropriate reactions.

Alongside these specific values, universal values also hold true for consumers. Values that apply to everyone, no matter what the target group. The influence that these have on an understanding of customer behaviour and prospective customer behaviour is probably greater than predictions made on the basis of target group descriptions. These are values that run through practically every customer group. They represent the 'ambiguous shopper' mentioned earlier. She will continually make choices (or no choices at all) based on her mood at that moment, in that situation and at that place, or in other words based on her needs within that particular context. Sometimes a customer is full of self confidence, sometimes the same customer is timid, sometimes she's in a hurry, at other times she has all the time in the world and sometimes it's raining – but often it isn't, and the sun is even shining when rain had been predicted.

A store will have to take all of these variables into account. No matter who the customer is, they will have an influence on him or her personally. Skilled personnel will be able to recognize certain frames of mind and play upon that, or a retailer can choose to fill this in with instore communications. You could even conceive of a formula that is specifically intended for a certain frame of mind (the traveller with not much time or the teenager who is seeking identification). It could also be an introduction to the translation of your brand on the Internet: namely, aimed at the needs and behaviour of a consumer at such an anonymous spot. For instance, when the consumer finds the threshold of the store too high, but would like to have the product.

Factors that influence the customer

In the Moment-Mood Model® the four factors that influence customer and prospective customer

⊕ MOMENT-MOOD MODEL®

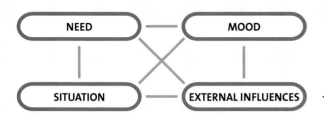

behaviour come together. All four are related to one another because they continually influence one another. Sometimes one will have the upper hand (a cheerful mood that is simply indestructible, for example), sometimes more factors are 'active' and different desires and moods will continually alternate, because of different situations, for instance.

Meaning of the four factors:

· *need*
  Is a person actually intent on buying a particular product? Or is he just getting oriented or shopping for fun or doing routine errands? Needs differ from one consumer to the other. Different needs often must be fulfilled side by side within a store.

· *mood*
  When someone is cheerful, he is receptive to very different things than when is he is depressed, stressed or sad. As a retailer you can capitalize upon alternating and very specific moods and thus try to influence buying behaviour. It shows that you understand the customer.

· *situation*
  The situation can often be taken advantage of excellently, by arranging everything very well

for the consumer. By his journey through the store and a well thought out service concept, for instance, but also by giving him just what he needs at the right moment. That way you can surprise a person, hold his attention and influence his mood in a positive manner.

· *external influences*
  All sorts of outside influences can have an effect on ultimate behaviour. These have an effect on a person's mood or needs. As Paco Underhill aptly puts it, "Every parking lot in the world has terrible weather all the time." The fact is, nothing can be done about these sorts of unpredictable factors. That is precisely the difference with situational factors, which can be played upon.

Customer behaviour can be better understood by acknowledging and recognizing these factors. Moreover, they also play a role in a customer's feeling of satisfaction or fulfilment after making a purchase. As you can probably imagine, a customer's good mood can turn into dejection when he becomes frustrated by a fruitless search for a particular product in a store. Or the other way around, if he has been helped more than expected because a member of the staff understood what his need was, he certainly will come back the next time.

Finally:
This model and line of reasoning is still relatively new and therefore not yet entirely worked out. It is, however, a fairly essential way of interpreting customer behaviour and what to do with that information. And even though it is not 'finished', in any event it will provide food for thought!

10
Differentiation

RIGHT PLACE, RIGHT MOMENT, RIGHT PROPOSITION

A brand has a personality equivalent to that of a person. Personal traits, values, rights and responsibilities can be ascribed to the brand. Brands can be arrogant, frugal or friendly. People expect brands to behave in certain ways and do not accept other ways of behaviour, just as they will say of friends and acquaintances: "That's so typical of him," or "That's not like him at all." "Oh, but it is!" says another.

Character, then, isn't what we think it is, or rather, what we want it to be. It isn't a stable, easily identifiable set of closely related traits, and it only seems that way because of a glitch in the way our brains are organized. Character is more like a bundle of habits and tendencies and interests, loosely bound together and dependent, at certain times, on circumstance and context. The reason that most of us seem to have a consistent character is that most of us are really good at controlling our environment.

Malcolm Gladwell (business and science journalist)

EXPECTED BEHAVIOUR

At such moments the only truth is the receiver's perception. Yet sometimes there are absolute truths, or a commonly accepted feeling about a person that is reputed to be the truth, for instance, that someone is trustworthy. In such a case the person must actually live up to that reputation, otherwise he falls short and is not taken seriously, or in this case, never trusted again.

By the time this happens with brands, the brand is only partially the possession of its owner. The brand has become public property, for the public has already dealt with the brand longer than its temporary management has. An example is Coca-Cola, which was dealt a severe blow by its users after it changed its recipe; ultimately the original recipe was reinstated and is now known in the United States as Coca-Cola Classic.

It was already mentioned earlier that a person

has the possibility of adapting to situations. Just as it's quite silly to step out of your tent during your vacation in three-piece grey and a tie, it's also unacceptable to go to a job interview wearing shorts and a T-shirt. The dress code, behaviour and language that you express can lead to success or failure, acceptation or rejection, being highly desired or shunned.

However, adapting does require a certain amount of subtlety in terms of the degree and manner of adaptation. Not everyone can be everything in a believable manner (at the drop of a hat) – and not everyone wants to be everything. There are people who avoid all controversy, who are not very self-confident or are even afraid, or are unambitious by nature and want to lead a quiet life. These people blend in with their environment, can adapt so well to their situation that they no longer are even noticed. But when progress and relevance is desired, it is important to be positively conspicuous, to display a certain amount of individuality in order to arouse interest. This is a balancing act between adapting and being different: 'standing out in the crowd'.

STANDING OUT IN THE CROWD

A brand has to stand out at all times, arouse a certain curiosity and come up with positive surprises. With product brands, this often will occur through innovative advertising, new products and product variations.

In stores, this comes about through a natural interplay of all elements of the formula. Retail formulas with a great number of stores often give them a uniform design and appearance because of logistic and economic considerations. From that point of view it seems economical, but over time this can cause major problems. What must you as a company do when you discover one day that you are no longer in tune with society? And that you have to adapt three or four hundred stores (and the logistics, the assortment, the personnel, maybe even more)?

The idea that a house style in the broadest sense of the word must be very rigidly implemented had been gradually drummed into the thinking of entrepreneurs. Because repetition would cause recognition and consequently preference with the end-user. This idea had initially been launched by architects, designers and advertising specialists – who in the first instance were quite right about it – and gradually, often going against the current, professionalized the world of brand thinking and doing. It's often forgotten, however, that along with the professionalization of that world, consumers have grown too. They have developed into skilled interpreters of signs and behaviour. The time is therefore ripe for a new mentality: the development of 'the brand' into a true personality. A stratified brand, that is, which can look differently and behave differently in different situations, depending on what is desirable in a given situation.

People sometimes forget that the consumer has developed along with the professionalization of the world.

That's why the possibility of brand stretch is so important. Perhaps not so much when the brand is at the peak of its fame, but there will come a day when a uniform one-dimensional brand will no longer have any pulling power. Just like with people, whom we find terribly boring when they have a very one-sided character and never show another, unexpected side.

McDonald's is in the danger zone. The overkill of 'always the same' is taking its toll. Moreover, the brand is so strongly associated with its assortment (fast food) that it does not even have one quick escape route in terms of products. Products that appeal more to healthy eating, for example. In an article about McDonald's, a dyed-in-the-wool McDonald's fan said: "I wouldn't trust it if

McDonald's suddenly started selling baguettes with Brie." And he's right!

Every country in the West has chain stores that are so monolithic and nationwide that they are an important, recognizable image in every city, town or village. In many cases they impose their house style mercilessly and try to stick their neon signs on every little building, no matter what its historical value. Granted, in terms of offer and price they certainly fulfil a great need, but the fact of the matter is that a certain uniform tastelessness is combined here with extensive nationwide coverage.

Brands, or rather 'clearly formulated identities', are the answer to a fragmented market. But in their desire for clarity they tend to become unambiguous and one-dimensional.

Guus Beumer
(manager of Designprijs Rotterdam, former SO art director)

That boring uniformity is partly the result of the enormously increased cost of the rents of A1 locations, so that small independent businesses with original store concepts no longer have a chance. But society is gradually changing. Local governments and zoning boards are making it a bit more difficult nowadays for the national chains to push through their uniformity. Although such retailers interpret this as government interference in the free market, in fact the government actually represents the spirit of the people – the people who are plain fed up with the same shopping streets everywhere throughout the nation.

· 'I've noticed just recently how dreary everything is in fact becoming. I don't really care for nationwide chains, their stores are always so ordinary.'
· 'Whether you shop in Groningen or Deventer, the exact same stores dominate the streets.'
· 'It no longer matters where you buy, you see the same brands everywhere.'

Interview with consumers on the street (Elsevier Retail)

The paradox is that such large chains as these are the ones who have the possibility of actually doing something with their capital. Something which may indeed require large investments, but which in the long run will yield more returns (and not only in terms of money). On the one hand, people will more easily accept further growth of the large chains because of such initiatives, and on the other hand, with the development of a broader representation the corporate personality will acquire several different facets. A personality with which they can approach the market in a more relaxed manner.

MULTIPLE INTERESTS

It is indeed pleasantly surprising when brands operate in several arenas and display different identities. High-end supermarket formulas such as Albert Heijn in the Netherlands, Carrefour in France, Tesco and Sainsbury in England, LobLaws in Canada and Wagman's in the United States are transforming the formulas of 'grocery shopping' by way of 'delicious and easy-to-prepare food' into 'easy living'. They now provide all sorts of extra services such as energy and money matters and have an obvious multiformat and multichannel strategy. Companies like Armani and Donna Karan have different lines of clothing, ranging from haute couture to ready-to-wear to jeans, and accordingly very different store formulas to match. They are becoming more and more involved with the lives of their customers, in the sense that they sell lifestyle products, magazines, music, scents and so forth, whether or not developed or designed by themselves. That versatility makes a good impression, is inspiring and shows that the company is busy with new developments and always right at the forefront of the market. The same goes for the supermarkets mentioned above.

The DKNY lifestyle store on Madison Avenue in New York

Mango displays its different looks on Oxford Street and Regent Street in London

The striking personality of Camper

MULTIPLE REPRESENTATIONS

The development of more differentiated physical stores can be achieved in various ways. The following is an ambitious approach: When several stores of one chain exist within a limited radius of action, it can be desirable to develop different representations purely from a visual standpoint. Like Mango in London, where three totally different outlets are located in Oxford Street, Regent Street and Neal Street.

Retail can be so boring. Look at Gap, it's the same everywhere you go. That's ridiculous, cities are completely different.

Shubankhar Ray (creative director of Camper)

And yet there is brand recognition through product, service and logo (used in totally different ways, for that matter). This form of retailing, which the Spanish shoe brand Camper also employs, adds sparkle to the brand. It conveys a certain feeling of pleasure and attentiveness to the customer; it is sympathetic and therefore goes above and beyond purely urging to buy.

A different line of approach can be helpful for retail formulas with many stores. They run a greater risk of acquiring an outdated image in the market on a massive scale. For these enterprises, it is advisable to maintain a continual state of development by means of a modular approach within the store

A brand is an interactive platform between kindred spirits. In the future it can no longer be one-dimensional.

concept, which introduces gradual adjustments throughout the entire chain. For example, a rear wall that bears the brand statement, which can be passed on from store to store every half year. Theoretically this would imply that it is superfluous to develop a 100% new concept. In actuality, the desire for real renewal will crop up from time to time anyhow, even if such a renewal will sooner be more evolutionary than revolutionary.

WHAT IS THE REALITY?

The first approach to differentiation draws heavily on the enterprise and entails high costs. Not so much the initial cost – which begins to play less of a role percentagewise in relation to the rise of rental prices at these locations – but it can become rather complicated in terms of administration.

The second approach to differentiation (modularity) is, considering our rapidly developing society, an inevitable development within modern retail and vitally important in the longer term. Here the store is subdivided both physically and intrinsically into separate concepts, which can be adapted or replaced per section. In supermarkets this can occur, for example, through the development of a 'ready to eat' concept, which consists of products and hardware that (at the cost of another product group, to be sure), can acquire a sort of shop-in-shop position at a strategic location in the store.

MULTIFORMAT/MULTICHANNEL

Besides various types of differentiation, real innovation will stem from multiformat/multichannel approaches. The formula adapts per situation with the proper image, proper assortment, proper location, and proper service, based on one strong (brand) personality.

We speak of a multichannel approach when a company offers its products or services through the Internet, direct marketing, call centres and the like, as well as in its physical stores. Many businesses have learned the hard way that the store formula cannot be copied into a virtual environment on a one-to-one basis. This is why a lot went wrong with the first Internet stores (and it still isn't simple to set up a profit-making concept). Every medium needs its own proposition, attuned to the needs of the consumer at that moment, at that specific place.

Becoming inspired or closing a deal on the Internet just happens to work differently than in a store. And even though specific desires will differ from person to person to a certain extent, you can still hook up to the larger movements reasonably well.

Albert Heijn is a good example of a completely filled in multiformat/multichannel strategy for this particular moment in time. They now have a neighbourhood store, a convenience store (AH ToGo), the normal Albert Heijn supermarkets (still the bulk of the operation), AH XL (a mega supermarket located on the outskirts of cities) and Albert (the Internet store of Ahold, in which Albert Heijn is one of the suppliers).

The different concepts focus fairly precisely on various types of user moments by means of a differentiated product and service package. The neighbourhood store as a real neighbourhood player, with lots of fresh and above all canned, packaged and frozen goods, aimed at single-person house-

Clockwise:
AH neighbourhood store;
'ordinary' AH;
AHXL,
AH ToGo

The multiformat strategy only succeeds if the consumer perceives the differences between the formats and considers them relevant.

holds or forgotten items on the grocery list. The atmosphere and staff also are part of the 'nearby' character of the proposition.

AH ToGo is a convenience store with freshly prepared warm and cold products for immediate consumption, a choice selection of instant and nearly instant meals and the 'absolutely indispensable forgotten grocery item'. The look and feel of the concept is urban and dynamic and indeed can be found in A1 urban locations and traffic interchanges such as petrol stations and train stations.

The normal Albert Heijn is a traditional supermarket with lots of fresh produce alongside the normal range of products that the average household requires on a weekly basis. Within this formula numerous product and category developments take place, which is essential for a top class formula and market leader.

The AH XL concept is superabundance: plenty of fresh produce, plenty of choice, but also bulk products for a better price. The concept is supplemented with hardware, amusement products, and various services such as financial affairs, dry cleaner, daycare and coffee shop. This is the store to visit once every two weeks, and it will take more time than usual, because the experience itself is

also what it's all about and practically considered a pleasant way of passing the time.

Ahold, the parent company of Albert Heijn, has a home delivery service, but is very strongly associated with the added value of the Albert Heijn brand in terms of service, courtesy, friendliness, etc. From the retail branding perspective, the distinction between the Ahold parent company and the Albert Heijn formula begins to fade here to a certain extent. The consumer is confronted with 'the company behind' their familiar Albert Heijn. Because of this large-scale aspect, the successes – but certainly also the disappointments – are made the most of in the media on the 'Ahold level'. This can easily cast a cloud on the relationship between the consumer and the once nearby grocer. With this the brand identity indeed goes through an almost imperceptible shift, one which is not easily reversed. That is neither good nor bad, but you certainly will have to take it into account when considering the position of the store formula.

CRATE & BARREL

Another example is the originally American chain Crate & Barrel, a home-furnishing store. They began with stores in city centres and shopping malls but have recently applied another strategy. They are now constructing buildings of their own architectural design near shopping centres because their personality comes across more clearly that way. In addition to this, they have outlet centres that have their own image within the existing identity and since recently a truly new formula which is more focused on a younger market – or in any case younger in spirit, less sedate. Crate & Barrel unleashed, as they themselves say. The formula is called CB2 and has a decidedly different look and feel without renouncing the identity of the brand. And of course sales are possible via the Internet and a catalogue. The brand radiates an obvious intelligence, as do the entrepreneurs.

Crate&Barrel with its personal architecture (Magnificent Mile as an example),
the Crate&Barrel outlet and the younger formula CB2.

Recognizability and authenticity on one hand, choice, inspiration and interactivity on the other, are the most important parameters for brands and their environments.

From product to service
From service to experience
From experience to meaning

INTELLIGENCE

On one side, multichannel and multiformat are ways of being able to realize more encounters with customers and potential customers by being where the customer is (location), with the right proposition (format – from flagship stores to simple stores to shop-in-shop), at the right moment (24 hours a day on the Internet, for instance). On the other side, the stratification and broader personality spectrum reveal the intelligence of the brand, which makes it a much more interesting partner for the customer in the longer term. For this is a brand that keeps up with the times in a natural and proactive manner. A suppleness of spirit, a suppleness of formula, steered by a strongly coordinated personality offers a brand the possibility of being and remaining relevant within the customer relationship, both now and in the future.

What such a multiformat/multichannel approach in fact offers is 'convenience' in the broadest sense of the word. It's all about making the consumer's search for goods and services as easy and pleasant as possible. Convenience doesn't always mean quick, but it does mean matching the frame of mind that the customer is in, or is induced into.

In their book The Experience Economy, Joe Pine and James Gilmore have already signalled that brands (product brands, retail brands and service brands) must develop from being suppliers of products into suppliers of experiences. We go a step further than that, because 'to experience' something is a rather consumerist, limited way of perceiving things. Take the Rainforest Café, for example: once you've been there three times, you've seen it, and you're ready for a new or bigger 'high'.

An intelligent brand can develop from being a supplier of products to 'a supplier' of service, then on to experience (following the reasoning of Pine and Gilmore) and finally to meaning. For only when a brand has and gives meaning is it destined to have a long future.

11
Retail Design

TRANSLATE THE LINE OF THOUGHT INTO MORE TANGIBLE MATTERS

Just as some people are very good at developing retail brand concepts, others are good at translating them into an actual situation. Ultimately, of course, we want a store formula that consists of tangible, visible, audible, tasteable and smellable elements. This is the terrain of retail design: inseparably connected with form and substance.

FROM WORDS TO IMAGES

We see that our Western world has changed immensely in the past 25 to 30 years. We used to be people of language and reason and now we need to have everything presented in visual images and short propositions. Design has assumed enormous proportions as a result. Design is the medium, the designer the doctor of spin.

Jos van der Zwaal beautifully described what retail design is and must do in an introduction to a lecture that I gave for a MA course in Design Management: "In modern Western society design has become as ubiquitous as air and water. We hardly notice it anymore, confrontations with highly innovative or mind bending examples excepted. A retail environment is the surrounding 'par excellence' where all functionalities of design are confronted with the public appreciation. Here design is challenged, tested and judged on its effectiveness without a jury, without a casebook and without mercy. The retail environment does not worry about academic divisions between graphic, interactive, product or environmental design. Here design just has to do its job. It has to be functional, physically as well as mentally. It has to communicate the targeted position and the quality level of the retailer. And it has to contribute to the reputation of the retail brand and the company behind it."

The fact that we are so visually oriented also emerged in the chapter on the Hong Kong Street. McDonald's yellow arches produce an immediate reaction in our minds. And nowadays we are no longer satisfied by just one medium at a time.

In a retail environment design is challenged, tested and judged on its effectiveness without a jury, without a casebook and without mercy.

Jos van der Zwaal (creative strategist)

The yellow arches, always recognizable everywhere

People don't have the patience to look at one TV channel, so we zap away as we read the newspaper with half an eye and send an SMS to a friend about where to meet tonight, turning on the computer in order to find a nice little restaurant. We might still long for the peace and quiet of a book, but we are too restless for that, and yet thankful for all these new media which make life so much easier.

The tremendously increased speed of daily life in Western society requires fast-paced acceptation, adaptation and appreciation. Which might make you wonder, what came first, the speed or our stepping of up the pace? Mahatma Gandhi once said that progress does not consist of 'increasing its speed'. No matter how nostalgic we might be at the thought of an unhurried, perhaps even rural life, what a short time we would be able to enjoy it, partly because of economic necessity, and partly because we would soon be overcome by boredom. The boredom that is always lying in wait just around the corner, making us constantly require new stimulants.

RETAIL: THE MIRROR OF SOCIETY

Retail, the mirror of our society, combats boredom and continually produces new stimulants, with design as the interpreter and visualizer. Rodney Fitch already said it back in 1990 in the introduction to his book *Fitch on Retail Design*: "Retail and design are both dynamic, so change and speed are important aspects of retail design. To maintain the necessary link between differing expectations of consumers and clients, retail design cannot be an 'art' as such, for comparative assessments and compromises are constantly necessary."

The dynamics of retail constantly require different and new physical solutions in order to be able to keep up with our changing needs and desires. Design not only gives shape to the imagination, but also shapes technical aspects, both in terms of the store (the customer journey) and manipulation (engineering). Fashion plays a great role in this, naturally. As was once said in an English fashion program about a dress, "One year you'll kill for it, the next year you wouldn't want to be caught dead in it." Fashion similarly plays an important role in retail design, with one branch of retail being more sensitive to fashion than another. In many cases this runs parallel to the difference between shop-

You'll see a shift to experiential and life-style shopping where the product will move away from the floor. People will go to the shops for the enjoyment, excitement and experience and may not physically buy at the shop, but may go away sensitised about some products and end up buying from the e-commerce front-end of the shop over the internet.

Jos van der Zwaal (creative strategist)

ping and running errands, but the changes in errand running are also steadily happening faster.

Retail, the mirror of our society, directly translates the general developments in our society into a form that it can use. In the book just mentioned written in 1990, Fitch elaborates on mail order shopping, call centres and television shopping channels, but said nothing about the Internet. Now, not even 15 years later, the Internet is inseparably connected with the multichannel strategy of almost every retailer.

The Harvard Design School Guide to Shopping devotes several chapters to the rise of the shopping mall (the first covered mall was erected in 1956), but also to the fall of the Shopping Mall phenomenon. By 1995, 12 million square feet were empty in the Chicago area alone. And according to the book, "By 2010, after the development of the requisite nonstore and virtual routes, 55% of the nation's shopping is predicted to be conducted in nonstore venues – online services, direct mail, catalogues, 800 numbers and the like."

In this context, Retail Design is the means for guiding the customer's journey, whether that be physical, virtual or otherwise. This is precisely what is illustrated in the Retail Choice Diagram®: the customer's journey from his sofa to his purchase. For each actual or virtual step, appropriate images, aids and incentives must be designed that suit the character of the supplier and are in keeping with one another.

Despite all the new developments and a decreasing amount of time spent on shopping, the physical store will remain part of the shopping landscape and of our daily surroundings. Yet stores will soon have to change for the better, for exciting alternatives offered by existing and new suppliers of experiential concepts are on the rise. These will easily attract a populace always looking for pleasure and relieve them of the money that they can only spend but once.

All that retailers *can* do is to create a strong brand personality in an inspiring environment for both people on the run and those who shop for fun.

One of our core philosophies is that we spend the money that other companies spend on marketing to create a store experience that exceeds people's expectations. We don't spend money on messages, we invest in execution.

Glen Senk (president of Anthropologie)

In every store you will encounter true 'on the run' and true 'fun' customers. The only thing is, distinguishing the difference between the two is difficult nowadays. For the customer who is purposefully looking for a product also wants the store to be a pleasant place. And the typical shopper wants to make her way through the store without too much difficulty. Moreover, people's moods can simply reverse, so that an errand runner suddenly becomes intrigued about a product and hangs around, and the shopper suddenly becomes a hurry to get the purchase over and done with. Stores must therefore always offer the possibility of being shopped in and appreciated at different tempos.

THE THREE PILLARS

Retail designers already play a role in the first route, which is more focused on the branding of the store.

During that analysis retail designers are capable of continually making a link between the hard facts and the visual images that correspond with those facts. In this way they provide a foundation that can be built upon further. Designers are the ones who make the dream come true. The following steps can be distinguished here:

· designing the idea
· designing the function
· designing the manipulability
· designing the feasibility
· designing the upkeep/the future

We have divided Retail Branding and Retail Design into what we call the three pillars:

⊕ THE THREE PILLARS®

BRAND IMAGE	RETAIL FUNCTION	OPERATIONAL SIDE
• strategic • long term • marketposition • market share • brand value	• tactical • improving retailfunction • attendancy index • conversion • receipt total	• economy of scale • cost control • efficiency • decisiveness • dynamics

The First Pillar: Brand Image

The first pillar involves the brand identity, which is expressed through the brand image. This is a strategic route for the long term. Here we take an extensive look at the identity, positioning and ambition of the enterprise. In addition we look for a new or renewed approach, or some sort of 'Big Idea'. How will the physical concept of the store operate, what will its visual representation be, and above all, how will it be different? Depending on the ambition, we then make a decision as to whether this step will be evolutionary or revolutionary.

The actual loading of the brand occurs by means of intangible values. Values that ultimately will be given tangible expression through an individual style, tone of voice and look and feel. The effect is market share and market value.

The Second Pillar: Retail Function

The second pillar involves the functional store route and is of a tactical nature. It deals with questions such as: How does the store work, what's the entrance like, the layout and routing, the allocation plan, the buildup within the departments, the presentation of the goods, the lighting (often underestimated, certainly in dressing rooms!), the graphics and general design, but also the 'backside of the store' (the logistical process, employee locales, etc.)? All of these together will provide the store experience and, in the end, the brand experience.

With an appropriate design you first want to get customers into the store. Next you want to keep them inside by means of a smooth flow through and between the departments, by inspiring product presentations and the pleasurable ambience of the store. Inspiration is the key word for everything that a company can do for its customers. In this regard, always give them more than they expect: more service, a new idea or a special/original sales campaign (which needn't necessarily be focused on price).

An inspiring environment with well-regulated customer flow is precisely what does wonders for conversion and the level of cash register receipts. Thus it's a matter of having the attraction value properly sorted out so that transaction can take place. (See the background information on attraction & transaction in chapter 2) The classic example of generating optimal customer flow is the escalator (see *Harvard Design School Guide to Shopping*). This suddenly made the floors on the upper levels effortlessly accessible, which had gigantic consequences for the level of receipts. People stayed longer, saw more and bought more.

For new solutions in regard to routing, department buildup and product presentation, it obviously holds true that the visual design must always coincide with the renewed or new elan of the company. The possibilities and freedoms that designers have at their disposal in this regard vary from company to company, are different for small stores than for large stores, and different again for discounters than for speciality stores – certainly in terms of the degree to which you can be truly innovative.

The Third Pillar: Operational Side

The third pillar concerns the operational route of the rollout, but also the daily functioning of the store. This involves feasibility, scale advantages, modularity, price control, and upkeep. All are elements in which the technical aspect of design is particularly important: knowledge of materials in terms of durability and cost, knowledge of systems, knowledge of construction projects and the processes involved in this.

In addition to this the daily dynamics of the store play a role: variety and change, possibilities for adaptation and the generation of incentives. This depends upon the branch, for as you can well imagine, an automobile tire specialist will have a lower visitor frequency than a department store. The former will logically require a lower rate of change and new incentives, yet both remain necessary. Designs for modules, presentation forms and, of course, means of instore communications are the most important aspects of this. Such elements often have a short lifespan. Materials and production methods should therefore be kept in proportion to that – an obligation to the costs of the operation and to our environment.

The three pillars provide insight into the evaluation of completed projects or subprojects, but are also meant to keep too-practically oriented entrepreneurs on their toes. They have a tendency to run ahead of things in reaction to brand questions and possible solutions and to claim that something is impossible or financially prohibitive. Each pillar has its own place within the route, its own corresponding approach and solution.

It is by innovating that brands remain relevant, justify their price premium and confirm their status as points of reference. Innovation is the lifeblood of a brand.

Jean-Noël Kapferer

DKNY in Soho New York, April '02 and Christmas '02. A different look through simple means

CONFORMING AND BEING DIFFERENT

With Retail Design there is a constant interplay between conforming and being different. Conformance is necessary because there are similarities within the branch that has to be recognizable for the consumer. For just like people, brands also maintain their existence by the grace of others. We compare ourselves with others and seek similarities in order not to fall out of the group; brands likewise position themselves in relation to other brands. Discounters look different than speciality shops, jewellers different than supermarkets and on a larger scale, shopping centres look different than outlet centres.

Top: Arkaden (Berlin); Bottom: Bataviastad (Lelystad, NL)
A luxury shopping centre and a (thematic) outlet centre

Conforming also means looking at how the competition does it, for similarities can make just as many things clear as differences. An article in the *Harvard Business Review* (2002) calls this 'choosing the right frame of reference': "Choosing the proper frame is important because it dictates the types of associations that will function as points of parity and points of difference."

For example, you will have to know what brands the competition carries and what you want to carry in addition to or contrast to that. The same goes for the services you offer, or the way in which you do your advertising. In the brown and white goods branch, for instance, it is customary to communicate by means of massive price advertising. If you don't do this, then it immediately looks as if you are aiming at the top segment of the market.

Being different is related to everything that has been previously discussed in this book. Being different puts you in a separate and recognizable place

Top: Loblaws (Toronto)
Bottom: Aldi (Rotterdam)

A high-end and a low-end supermarket, obviously different obviously supermarkets

in the market; coupled with your personality, it makes you eligible. Distinction is the motive behind every renewal and innovation. And renewal and innovation is the only way of maintaining your position.

Disney store in Paris in Oct. '02 in white and silver; next to that the store from Oct. '01 is entirely outdated

THE PROCESS IS THE PRODUCT

The process is the product (it's a never ending story). A retail formula is always developing in interaction with changes in society and with the contemporary person's constant need for change. Moreover, in chapter 10 on differentiation the point was also raised that in the present day and age it is neither handy nor desirable to roll out a formula in a uniform house style. The founder of the English fashion chain Oasis once said: "I don't want to wake up one morning with 100 outdated stores." There he hits the nail on the head.

Concept and design must be constantly checked for contemporaneity of form and content, for recognizability and surprise, for the needs of the consumer and the possibilities of the employees, the front and the back. The modular approach is a solution for slowing down the fleeting, transitory nature of the physical representation. The idea of

the timeless store is an *idée fixe*, but a longer life through sectional changes on a continual basis is indeed attainable and desirable. Design is the key to attainability and to the success of a planned longer life.

Design is the wellspring of branding. Great design takes guts and is soul deep.

Tom Peters

DESIGNERS

The designer as the prima donna for the commercial retail business is not an option. (Leaving aside the exceptions like Paul Smith, Donna Karan and Terence Conran who behave more as entrepreneurs.) Design must be part of an organization's Brand and Retail Development Team, as it were, as described in the Platform Development® model. Successful retail is a team effort and not a piece of art.

Design is becoming less and less optional. It's becoming a requirement. This is because branding has become inescapable, and taking care of your brand means you constantly have to watch it, continually have to maintain it. What used to last five years now lasts one year at most.

Adrian Warren (associate marketing director of River Island)

12

Retail Complexity

THE COHERENCY OF EVERYTHING

Branding creates a world, a world that takes its shape through physical expressions. Retail branding tells the story of the company, whereby the company takes its shape through physical expressions.

The conceptual world of product brands is of a different order than the down-to-earth world of retail brands. Everything is possible in the world of products, where we can just as easily enjoy an ice cream cone on a deserted island with white beaches and swaying palm trees as we can take pleasure in a cigarette, imagining ourselves to be a tough cowboy in the Grand Canyon. The real world behind the façade only comes to life when something goes wrong. For example, when people become sick from that ice cream, the company behind it suddenly comes in direct contact with the users.

The world of retail operates in the here and now. There is a direct relationship between the company, its personnel and the consumers. The true nature of the company can be experienced in all aspects, both the rational elements (what you do and what you offer) and the emotional elements (who you are and how you do it). Therefore the physical expressions of a company must be coupled with its underlying values, ambitions and possibilities.

That is the essence of this book. In this last chapter we want to emphasize the holistic concept upon which it is based. Therefore we will take a second look at all of the models dealt with separately in the previous chapters and attempt to explain the coherency of everything.

THE COHERENCY OF THE MODELS

Our work is about renewing retail formulas, giving them a facelift and bringing them up to date. But you cannot make a start without a good foundation. The first model, The Retailformula® (in chapter 3, Identity), sheds light on that foundation. It reveals how the core of the brand and the realization of the

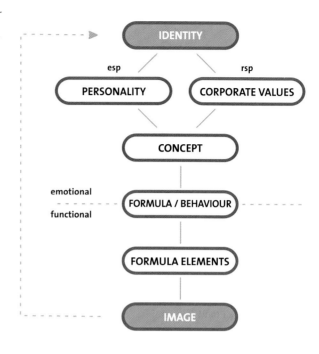

⊕ THE RETAIL FORMULA®

concept relate to the total operational store formula. At one glance you can see the relationship between the identity of the company and its image in the market. The identity is equally built up out of rational and emotional propositions, and the image arises from the perceivable physical elements, the marketing P's. This makes it obvious that insight and knowledge about the personality aspects of the company are indispensable, seeing as this basically determines half of the success or failure of the retail formula. Therein lies the limitation perhaps, but certainly the strength as well. And for us, the challenge – for an equal balance between emotional and rational values is certainly not yet common within today's business world.

Vision and/or ambition are the motivating forces behind new steps. Together with identity and positioning they give direction to concepting. And therefore these three can be found at the top of the Brand In Your Hand® model. This model was discussed in chapter 9 on Retail Renewal and Retail Innovation, as it is a guideline for concepting. Concepting broadens the vision of the possibilities of the retail branding in relation to the target group. In many cases these possibilities extend much further than the core business – and that gives thinking room, continuity and a vision of the future. An added plus is that this kind of thinking gives a tremendous impetus to the company and all of its employees, because people find it stimulating to be busy with the future.

The motives behind the decision to undergo renewal will be different for every company. An outmoded interior, a broadening or change of the product line, adapting to the times, etc. However, when one component of the store formula is fundamentally changed, it will be necessary to consider the effect of that change on all the other elements of the formula. In many cases, in fact, a seemingly small change will have huge consequences for the entire operation. Those consequences not only extend to the elements visible in the store, but can also effect the operational side of the retail formula. A remark by Vittorio Radice, the man who helped the English department store Selfridges out of the morass and made it a booming business again, threw a clear light on this matter: "There was no point refurbishing the store, if we didn't refurbish the way we did business."

⊕ BRAND IN YOUR HAND®

The Platform Development® model graphically portrays this viewpoint. It is an important next step in the process, because it charts the current situation and the steps that must be taken in order to realize the concept. Without wanting to underplaying the importance of this model, we will not go into it any further at this point, for it has already been discussed in great detail in chapter 7.

⊕ PLATFORM DEVELOPMENT®

formula concept / ambition

Meanwhile, we have now come to the more concrete interpretation of the renewed retail formula. After having thought out, described and imagined the concept, the real designing of elements and sub-elements can begin. Although the concept is 'the dream' and adjustments are sometimes deemed necessary, this is a document that contains all of the important starting points and you will see that those starting points seldom change as long as a business does not drastically readjust its ambitions. And of course this mustn't take years, for by then the spirit of the times will have changed again, so that the positioning might no longer be relevant. For in a store formula the behaviour of the enterprise is adapted to the times of the society. Remember that 'Retail reflects society'.

Until now we have primarily focussed on the first of the three cornerstones discussed in the previous chapter, the Brand Image, which is responsible for brand value and market share. The visual and physical design of the formula can indeed only be successful when there is a tremendous amount of knowledge and understanding about the essence of the company. But that alone will not lead to a satisfactory store concept. The second cornerstone, Retail Functionality, leads to a layout and store makeup that matches the identity and desired image perfectly. This cornerstone ensures the commerciality of the concept. The third cornerstone, Operations, involves the feasibility of the implementation, the economy of scale, the strength and the necessary dynamics.

All three are of a different order, but form an inseparable whole. Experience shows that it is necessary to consider these cornerstones both separately and in combination. In combination because the connection between elements forms a holistic aggregate here too. They are interwoven with each other in such a way that all three are equally important, and if they are to form a strong foundation all three must be equivalent in quality and size. And separately because they are of a different kind and substance, which requires a concentrated, specialized approach in order to be developed.

⊕ THE THREE PILLARS®

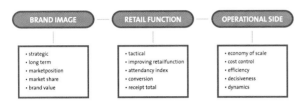

Retailers are people of the moment in the sense that they react directly to market conditions. This has always been their strength. Yet the most successful retail formulas are young; a good many older ones have vanished because even though they did often react directly to the market they displayed little strategic vision. That strategic vision is particularly dealt with in the first cornerstone, where there is not only an analysis of the personality and how it should develop, but also the contemporary relevance for the market and employees (and to a somewhat lesser extent, for the direct interests of shareholders).

The above-mentioned models are all aimed at attracting and inspiring the consumer, but they probably appear to have been conceived to a great extent from the point of view of the enterprise, as if that were the leading player in the market situation. But it is the consumer who ultimately determines what is and is not successful. Yet our line

of approach is that you cannot actually create something for a supposed target group. The idea is to operate from your own brand personality. That personality distinguishes you and makes you more eligible than others. In spite of this, the last model shows that the consumer indeed is the leading factor for many decisions. The Retail Choice Diagram® (see chapters 5 and 6) illustrates the road that the consumer must follow in order to buy an arbitrary product. In a manner of speaking, this model turns the whole thing upside down and is perhaps the most important guideline for gaining insight into how the store formula and the purchasing process works. What it essentially comes down to is that while a consumer is at home thinking of a product she wants to buy, she spontaneously puts the company on her shortlist. In doing so, she sees a virtual picture of the physical store, perhaps even the street, and the shelf in the store. Next she takes those steps in actuality and the storekeeper will have to meet her expectations each step of the way – or rather, surpass them. That's why the Retail Choice Diagram® can also be used as a checklist for the retailer, as all steps must be completed in relationship to one another.

The endpoint of the exercise is the new or renewed retail design. In the best case, retail design makes the dream come true or comes as close as possible to doing so. On the one hand it represents the identity in all aspects of the formula and on the other it creates the proper routing, sight lines, shelf plans, and so forth, developed within economic and commercial frameworks.

It should be clear that the development of a store formula, which ultimately grows into a brand, is a team effort whereby many disciplines – very many, in some cases – play a role. That's why it is so important to keep focusing on the coherency of all those disciplines, and on the starting point and the final objective, but above all on the road itself. These models are very useful tools in this regard. They provide room for contemplation of the most important goal: the creation of inspiring, innovative concepts that give the consumer real service with a smile.

⊕ RETAIL CHOICE DIAGRAM®

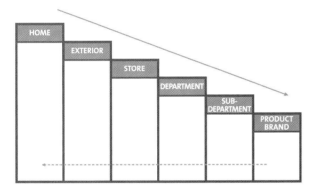

I believe that things have to look simple and be simple – for the customer, at least. But there is no simple way to achieve that; you have to go through it all.

A FINAL WORD

Brands exist by grace of the relevance that they bring to the target group. A relevance that is based on the unique underlying values of the brand – who the brand is, what the brand does and how the brand works in the here and now. If people can identify with those unique emotional and rational values, the brand will be successful.

People focus on the future and expect such future orientation from their brands as well, which is why continuous innovation is of vital importance.

A retail brand must be even more real than a product brand because in contrast with product brands, people in store environments actively encounter the brand and each other and experience it as true. And hopefully value it.

A brand needs a foundation and a future; it is our task to pave the way as the brand steers its daily course between them, but also to keep it interesting and exciting.

Michel van Tongeren
Amsterdam

REFERENCES

Books

Akkermans, Don A.M. *Goedendag, ik ben de nieuwe eigenaar van uw beeldmerk.*
Deventer, NL: Kluwer bedrijfwetenschappen, 1992.

Bedbury, Scott. *A New Brand world.*
New York: Viking Penguin, 2002.

Boer, Ruud. *Brand Design.*
Amsterdam: Pearson Education Benelux, 2003.

Conran, Terence. *Leven met design.*
Weert, NL: Van Buuren Uitgeverij BV, 1999.

Conran, Terence. *Terence Conran on Restaurants.*
London: Conran Octopus Limited, 2000.

Conran, Terence. *Terence Conran's new House Book.*
London: Guild Publishing, 1985.

Crawford, Fred & Ryan Mathews.
The Myth of Excellence.
New York: Crown Business, 2001.

Din, Rasshied. *New Retail.*
London: Conran Octopus Limited, 2000.

Fitch, Rodney & Lance Knobel. *Fitch on Retail Design.*
Oxford: Phaidon Press Limited, 1990.

Franzen, Giep & Marieke van den Berg. *Strategisch Management van Merken.*
Deventer, NL: Kluwer, 2002.

Gladwell, Malcolm. *Het Omslagpunt*
(The Tipping Point).
Amsterdam/Antwerp: Uitgeverij Contact, 2001.

Howard, John A. *Buyer Behavior in Marketing Strategy*, 2nd ed.,
New Jersey, USA: Prentice Hall International, 1994.

Kapferer, Jean-Noël. *Strategisch Merkmanagement*,
2nd ed. (Les Marques, Capital de l'Enterprise).
Schoonhoven, NL: Academic Service, 1996.

Kapferer, Jean-Noël. *(Re)inventing the brand*
(Ce qui va changer les marques).
London: Kogan Page Limited, 2001.

Kralingen, Roland van. *Superbrands.*
Deventer, NL: Samson, 1999.

Kralingen, Roland van. *Brand World.*
Eindhoven, NL: Kluwer, 2002.

Kotler, Philip. *Marketing Management*, 9th ed.,
New Jersey, USA: Prentice Hall International, 1997.

Lubbe, Jan C.A. van der & Aart J.A. van Zoest.
Teken en Betekenis.
Bloemendaal, NL: Aramith Uitgevers, 1997.

Macrae, Chris. *The Brand Chartering Handbook.*
Essex, UK: Addison-Wesley Longman, 1996.

Mitchell, Alan. *Right Side Up.*
London: Harper Collins Publishers, 2001.

Olins, Wally. *Corporate Identity.*
London: Thames & Hudson, 1989.

Olins, Wally. *The new Guide to Identity.*
Hampshire, UK: Gower Publishing Limited, 1995.

Peters, Tom. *De Innovatiecirkel*
(The Circle of Innovation).
Amsterdam/Antwerp: Uitgeverij Contact, 1998.

Project on the City 2. *Harvard Design School Guide to Shopping.* Cologne: Taschen, 2001.

Pine, Joseph & James Gilmore.
The Experience Economy.
Boston: Harvard Business School Press, 1999.

Ries, Al & Jack Trout. *Positionering* (Positioning).
Alpen aan den Rijn/Diegem, NL: Samson
Bedrijfsinformatie, 1996.

Riewoldt, Otto. *Retail Design.*
Amsterdam: BIS Publishers, 2000.

Rijkenberg, Jan. *Concepting.*
The Hague: Uitgeverij BZZTôH, 2001.

Roothart, Hilde. *Trendslator Brain Kit.*
Trendslator, © 2001.

Schmitt, Bernt H. & Alex Simonson.
Marketing Aesthetics.
New York: The Free Press, 1997.

Schmitt, Bernd H. *Experiential Marketing.*
New York: The Free Press, 1999.

Ster, W van der & P.J. van Wissen. *Marketing & Detailhandel*, 4th ed.,
Groningen, NL: Wolters-Noordhoff, 1987.

Oordt, Marjolijn van. *Superbrands Nederland, Het successverhaal van 40 topmerken in Nederland.*
London: Superbrands Ltd., 2001.

Underhill, Paco. *Why We Buy.*
New York: Simon & Schuster, 1999.

Williams, Gareth. *Branded?*
London: V&A Publications, 2000.

Zwaal, Jos van der. *Design voor opdrachtgevers*, 2nd ed.,
Amsterdam: Uitgeverij BIS, 2000.

Articles

Anderson, Stephen. "The World of the Retailer."
International Lighting Review, 2000.

van Amerongen & van der Geest. "Retail en branding." *stedebouw & architectuur*, 4, 2002.

Baltesen, Frits. "Albert Heijn profiteert van reizende consument."
NRC Handelsblad, 30-10-2002.

Bird, Michael. "Brain Power."
In-store Marketing, May 2002.

Bluiminck, Nathalie.
"Thema's naar je eigen bedrijf vertalen."
Bakkerswereld (Elsevier Food), 19-09-2002.

Booth, Hannah. *"The Next Step."*
Design Week, 31-10-2002.

Bosveld, Karin. Giep Franzen interviews Asher Cohen: "De verzonnen geschiedenis van River Island."
Tijdschrift voor Marketing, February 2000.

Bosveld, Karin. "Breaker kan misschien wel een iMac worden." Tijdschrift voor Marketing, June 2002.

Bottler, Stefan. "Die Macke macht's." *Werben & Verkaufen*, 43, 2001.

Brady, Rupert Parker. article on Hans Benshop: "Het zit me hoog, hè?!" *RetailTribune*, 14-09-2000.

Brandmeyer, Klaus. article on his presentation at the BrandGenetics Symposium: "Het merk als business driver." 20-09-2002.

Bruijn, Peter de. *"Dood aan het merk*, Naomi Kleins manifest tegen het wereldkapitalisme."
NRC Handelsblad, 16-02-2001.

Buiten, Luberto van. Nicholas Ind on Internal Branding: "Internal branding stimuleert merkperceptie van consument."
NieuwsTribune, 30-05-2002.

Capell & Khermouch & Sains. "Hip H&M."
Business Week, 11-11-2002.

Cushman & Wakefield. Healey & Baker research: "Nederlander geen 'echte' funshopper."
Detailhandel Magazine. May 2002.

Doggers, Robert. "Merken zoeken lijfelijk contact met jongeren." *Parool*, 23-08-2002.

Dröge, Philip. "Shop Till You Drop." QPF 2, 2002.

Engelsen, Bram den. "De medewerker als merkbouwer." *Tijdschrift voor Marketing*, October 2002.

Erdbrink, Thomas. "Ook als het oorlog is, feest Dubai." *NRC Handelsblad*, 28-12-2002.

FHV/BBDO. "Retailmerken in ontwikkeling" a report.

Frölke, Victor. "Niet zo happy meer bij McDonald's." NRC Handelsblad 14-11-2002.

Gelder, Sicco van. "A view on the future of Branding." Brand Meta, © April 2002.

Gelder, Sicco van. "Branding op wereldschaal." Tijdschrift voor Marketing, October 2002.

Gianotten, Henk. "Creatie van klantwaarde." *Detailhandel Magazine*, January 2001.

Gommer & Heijmans. "Strategisch communicatie-middel thema designmanagement." *Design in Business*, March 1998.

Gons, Piet Hein. "De consument is dood, leve de prosument." *Adformatie*, 04-01-2001.

Gremmen, Paul. "Ritueel kicken tussen de grote merken." *Adformatie*, 13-12-2002.

Groothengel, Paul. "Branding binnenstebuiten." *Adformatie*, 29-08-2002.

Harvest Communications LLC. "Lessons from Cultural Icons: How to create an Iconic Brand." Harvest Communications LLC, © 2002.

Haveman, Frank. "Dichter bij de nieuwe werkelijkheid." *Tijdschrift voor Marketing*, February 2002.

Heijden, Toine van der. "Het merk is dood. Leve het merk!" *Management Team*, 05-10-2001.

Heijden, Toine van der. "Jonge merken." *Management Team*, 04-11-2001.

Heijden, Toine van der. "De toekomst van het merk." *Management Team*, 02-12-2001.

Horn, Iris. "Lang leve het puppy." *Adformatie*, 18-01-2001.

Hospes, Cor. "Buiten winnen, is binnen beginnen." *Adformatie*, 14-12-2001.

Hurts, Floris. "Serviceconcepten maken de dienst uit." *NieuwsTribune*, 06-06-2002.

Jong, Nico de. "Saaier op straat. Consumenten ergeren zich aan eentonige winkelstraten." *Elsevier Retail*, June 2002.

Jong, Nico de. "Spiedende ogen." *Elsevier Retail*, October 2002.

Jong, Nico de. "Het vlakke land." *Elsevier Retail*, December 2002.

Keller, Sternthal & Tybout. "Three questions you need to ask about your brand." *Harvard Business Review*, September 2002.

Kessels, Jan. "Na de e-commerce hype is branding het buzz word." *RetailTribune*, 08-05-2001.

Koelewijn, Rinskje. "Een Yes-meisje wil het liefst heel gewoon zijn." *NRC Handelsblad* 20-11-2001.

Kohnstamm, Max. "Sterke merkidentiteit dekt dakschade." *Adformatie*, 19-09-2002.

Koning, Josee. "Leercurve is afgerond bij Etos." *RetailTribune*, 08-03-2001.

Krooshof, Thecla. "Oppervlakkigheid van merken is vaak hun kracht." *EYE Zicht op trends*, September 2002.

Kruisselbrink, Erik. Michel van Tongeren on bakeries: "De handtekening van de bakker moet je in de winkel zien." *Elsevier Bakkerswereld*, 25-11-1999.

Lammers, Cindy. "Are you experienced?" *Adformatie*, 15-12-2000.

Libbenga, Jan. "Merk wordt winkel, winkel wordt merk." *NRC Handelsblad*, 07-05-2002.

Lier, Bas van. "Merkkleding." *Adformatie*, 06-12-2001.

Maathuis, Rodenburg & Sikkel. "Geloofwaardigheid van merken: verstand en gevoel." *Tijdschrift voor Marketing*, July-August 2002.

Munk, Kirsten. "Mikken op de hele familie." *Adformatie*, 30-05-2002.

Pegtel, Alies. "Shoe-shopping is beter dan seks." *Carp*, June 2002.

Postema, Kees. "Herkenbaarheid design bevordert merkentrouw." *NieuwsTribune*, 8-11-2001.

Reesch, Koos van. article on Christiaan Rikkers: "Teveel schitterend ontworpen winkels zijn in schoonheid gestorven." *InStore* 3, 2001.

Rhode, Carl. article on John Grant, author of After Image: "De consumptiemaatschappij van de vorige eeuw gaf plezier en maakte dom." *Tijdschrift voor Marketing*, December 2002.

Riezebos, Rik. "Internal Branding: medewerkers zijn het merk." *Tijdschrift voor Marketing*, June 2002.

Roothart, Hilde. "Hard tegen hard." *Tijdschrift voor Marketing*, December 2002.

Schaafsma, Coraline. "Merk moet leiden tot betekenisvolle relatie." *EYE Zicht op trends*, September 2002.

Schrameijer, Hugo. "Marketingwereld heeft amper oog voor winkelvloerpromoties." *Tijdschrift voor Marketing*, June 2002.

Segers, Rien (interviewed). "Hoogtijdagen van branding zijn voorbij." *Adformatie*, 15-11-2001.

Slierings, Ruud. "Het verschil tussen bereiken en beroeren." *FD KLM*, March 2000.

Slooten, Ruud van. article on Guus Beumer: "Vroeger moest het image een identiteit represen- teren, nu kan het image tientallen identiteiten zijn." *MAN*, date unknown.

Smit & van den Berg. "Een merk in mensentermen." *Tijdschrift voor Marketing*, June 2002.

Smit, Richard. "Een romantisch verlangen Merken op zoek naar authenticiteit." *Adformatie*, 31-08-2000.

Smit, Richard. "Boodschappen bij de boodschappen." *Adformatie*, 21-09-2000.

Smit, Richard. "Vendex KBB en het branding-spelletje 'Ik ben een bofkont.'" *Adformatie*, 20-12-2001.

Spinhoven, Josje. "Pratende schappen en hippe tassen." *Retail Week* 49, date unknown.

Stamsnijder, Paul. "Belofte maakt schuld." *NieuwsTribune*, 25-07-2002.

Stroeken, Jack. "Japan blijft het land van oplossingen en innovaties." *EYE Zicht op trends*, May 2002.

Swarte, Gijs de. article on Fred A. Crawford: "Je moet niet overal goed in willen zijn." *Adformatie*, 10-05-2002.

Terwindt, Robin. "Merkenbouw met reuzen- sprongen." *NieuwsTribune*, 21-06-2001.

Thorborg, Lia. "Eerst het merk, dan de producten." *Ondernemen!*, July 2000.

Toffler, Alvin & Heidi, "Nieuwe Economie? Dit was nog maar het begin." *NRC Handelsblad*, 27-04-2001.

Verhoeven & Slot. "De Lokroep van het winkel- centrum." *Safe*, date unknown.

Veul, Connie. "De kern van het merk." *NieuwsTribune*, 23-11-2000.

Visser, Harm. "Het hoofd is waar het hart is." *Adformatie*, 06-12-2001.

Vlam, Peter. "Web & Winkel." *Adformatie*, 23-11-2001.

Vlemmings, Marc. "Het merk is geen religie." *Identity Matters*, June 1999.

Vugt, Theo van. article on Marc de Swaan Arons van EffectiveBrands: "Een verkeerde definitie van een markt leidt tot verzadiging." *Tijdschrift voor Marketing*, June 2002.

Werkhoven, Phaedra. "Henk Schiffmacher, schilder en 'tattoo king' over het leven en de herinneringen op zijn lijf." *Carp*, 02-07-2002.

Wiering, Connie. "Van Trends naar Brands." *Tijdschrift voor Marketing*, January 2002.

Wiering, Connie. article on retail researcher Paco
Underhill: "Echte retailmanagers hebben geen leren
zolen." *Tijdschrift voor Marketing*, December 2002.

Websites

www.adformatie.nl

www.brand.com

www.branddating.nl

www.brandhome.com

www.beyondtheline.nl

www.eim.nl

www.envirosell.com

www.eye.nl

www.faithpopcorn.com

www.hbd.com

www.jrcanda.com

www.marketing-online.nl

www.media-exposure.nl

www.mt.nl

www.retailindustry.com

www.rmc.nl

www.samhoud.nl

www.visualstore.com

www.warc.com

www.zibb.nl

COLOPHON

BIS Publishers
Herengracht 370-372
1016 CH Amsterdam
T 0031 20 524 7560
F 0031 20 524 75 57
www.bispublishers.nl
bis@bispublishers.nl

© 2003 Michel van Tongeren, Amsterdam
ISBN 90 6369 043 6

Author: Michel van Tongeren, Amsterdam
Design by: Ron van Roon and Meike Jürgens,
Amsterdam
Translation by: Jane Bemont, Amsterdam
Printed by: TWP, Singapore